BEYOND THE TIMBERLINE

**The
Trials and Triumphs
of a
Black Entrepreneur**

Theodore Martin (T.M.) Alexander, Sr.

M.E. Duncan & Company, Inc., <u>Publishers</u>

We gratefully acknowledge the contributions of Janice A. Davis, *A Legacy of Service and Commitment;* Rev. Otis Moss, Jr., D.D., *Open Letter to T.M. Alexander, Sr.;* the late John A. Sibley, *Foreword*; the children and grandchildren of T.M. Alexander, Sr., for excerpts from *The Things I Said To Me I Say To You; The Atlanta Constitution* and *The Atlanta Journal* for permission to reprint the "Griffin article"; and, Lloyd's, London for a reprint of Lloyd's Policy for churches of Montgomery, Alabama.

M.E. Duncan & Company, Inc., <u>Publishers</u>
Edgewood, MD 21040   (410-538-5579)

Editorial process: Staff of M.E. Duncan & Company, Inc.

Library of Congress Catalog Card Number: 92-71604

Alexander, Sr., Theodore Martin (T.M.), 1909-
   Beyond The Timberline - The Trials and Triumphs of a Black
   Entrepreneur

1. Alexander, Sr., Theodore Martin (T.M.), 1909-   2. Insurance--
United States--Biography. 3. Real Estate -- United States--Biography.
4. African-American business enterprises-History-20th Century.
5. Executives--United States--Biography. 6. Atlanta, Georgia-History-
20th Century.   -Index-

ISBN 1-878647-08-3

First printing, November 1992
5 4 3 2 1

Dedication

To Young People
All Over the
World

To those who wish to rise above the narrow confines of race and the crippling influence of prejudice.

OLIVET INSTITUTIONAL BAPTIST CHURCH
8712-14 QUINCY AVE
CLEVELAND, OHIO 44106

The Reverend Otis Moss JR., D.D.
    PASTOR

September 30, 1981

Mr. T.M. Alexander, Sr.
Washington, D.C.

Dear "Uncle Alex":

When the great poet said, "God, give us men times like these demand; strong arms, great hearts, true faith, and ready hands," he had to have had men like you in mind.

Fifty years ago when you began your business, there was no modern Civil Rights Bill on the books, no Voting Rights Act, no Supreme Court decisions to protect, sustain, maintain, or defend your rights, needs, interest, hopes, dreams, and aspirations.

When you dared adventure to build a business that has already lasted half a century, there were no Affirmative Action plans, minority set-asides, SBAs, OMBEs, UDAGs, Economic Development Acts, and Block Grants to pull, push, or cheer you on.

You had an Old Testament prophetic tenacity, a New Testament sense of character and service, plus the legacy of praying parents.

Your vocation, profession and dedication have outlived Mussolini's Italy, Hitler's Germany, Franco's Spain, Crump's machine, Talmadge's Terror, Biblo's brutality, and Wallace's wickedness. Your family has to love you, your friends must admire you, and your enemies have to respect you.

Edwina and our children join me in a signal salute to you and your record of excellence and accomplishments.

Special congratulations to Lenora, your beloved and charming wife who brings brilliance, grace, dignity, and efficiency to her position in the U.S. Labor Department.

                Yours in admiration and respect,
                Reverend Otis Moss, Jr.

CHAPTERS
IN THE LIFE OF
T.M. Alexander, Sr.

Chapters

Acknowledgments

While I have had a great deal of success from a material standpoint, I have always felt it was guided, blessed from a divine source. I knew from an early age I wanted to be in business.

My family were serious church people and I grew up in Dexter Avenue Baptist Church in Montgomery, Alabama. Later, I attended college where I met Howard Thurman, an inspiring dean at Morehouse College. I achieved some academic success in my course of study at Morehouse which was mainly Business Administration, but also included English Literature, and Political Science.

Thurman, however, achieved success for just being himself and even during my college days, he was considered a mystic. I can recall almost verbatim some of his performances. His words meant as much to me as those guiding Christian principles my mother and father taught me. But it is from Howard Thurman that I adopted a motto, of sorts, to describe my activities as a businessman in Atlanta - *Beyond the Timberline*. This was the title to one of Thurman's more famous parables that expresses the tenor of my life's efforts.

While a student, Chapel was compulsory, and usually we always tried to find a means to avoid it unless it was known that Thurman was to preach. I remember his riveting words, the sincerity of his being, and the ethical and philosophical teaching he supplied to us all at Morehouse. There would scarcely be a vacant seat on such occasions. I was honored to have him as my friend. He was so convincing, so sincere in every way.

Foreword

by John A. Sibley

"Fellowship" is the word which T.M. Alexander, Sr., uses to describe his relationship with his friends. My respect and friendship for him arose some thirty years ago when a number of White businessmen formed a corporation to provide resources for Blacks who wished to purchase homes or occupy apartments.

The man chosen to fulfill the building of the homes and apartments was T.M. Alexander, Sr. He accepted the task and together with his associates employed engineers, architects, and builders, and sold or rented the units built. Under this arrangement, T.M. and his group built and sold 203 homes on two tracts of land having a value at the time of sale of more than $5,800,000 and built an apartment with 127 units, in the center of the Atlanta University complex: a much-needed resource for faculty and guests. The funds advanced by the corporation were all repaid in full and Mr. Alexander and his associates operated profitably.

The first two projects had no financial needs except the seed money which was the purchase price of the property to be developed. Not so with respect to the apartment buildings which required additional credit. This was arranged by the local banks putting up the construction financing and by the Atlanta Civic Enterprises accepting liability for the venture capital beyond the difference between the permanent loan and the cost of the building.

This was a pioneering venture that established long-term financing for the Black community which had never before been available to them, to my knowledge.

During this period of time, the successful completion of the homes and apartments was a Herculean accomplishment, and for this, T.M. earned the respect and confidence of both Black and White businessmen within the city.

During the course of Mr. Alexander's work on this project, we met frequently. I came to admire his intelligence, character, ability, and courage. I learned of his continuing activity in civic affairs. He had been Chairman of the Board of the Butler Street YMCA and Vice-Chairman of the Advisory Committee of the Better Housing Commission of Atlanta.

His primary business interest has always been in property insurance, and he has achieved wide recognition for his acumen, expertise, and fair dealing. I count myself fortunate in having had the opportunity to know him and to see at first hand the cordial cooperation which he brought to all of those with whom he worked. His gift of bringing the quality of fellowship to whatever he undertook and the use of his talents in exemplifying and promoting cooperation between Whites and Blacks in both business and civic affairs has set an example for the leaders, both Black and White, of Atlanta.

John A. Sibley

John A. Sibley, deceased, was a long-time acquaintance of T.M. Alexander, Sr. During Sibley's life, he had been a Baldwin County judge, attorney for Coca-Cola, and chairman of Trust Company Bank. In 1961, in public forums across the State of Georgia, Mr. Sibley helped defuse the threatening massive resistance tactics brewing because of implementation of Brown vs. Board of Education, which demanded desegregation of public schools. An editor of *The Atlanta Constitution* said, "The Sibley Commission was the pivotal force that created the climate in which politicians could act to save public education in the state."

Introduction
Reflections of a Life Well Spent

I used to say, jokingly, that when I woke up one day and found that I had been born in the cradle of the Confederacy, I kicked the slats out of my own cradle and left Montgomery, Alabama with no desire to return. This is not quite true, however, and even if we could choose the place and circumstances of our birth, as Blacks we would be hard-put to choose a place free of the agonizing problems which the accident of birth imposed upon us.

We were, and still are, between the "rock and the hard place." Either we succumbed to the debilitating effects of segregation or chose to develop a method for survival and success. I always wanted to do the latter; that did not come easy.

I agree with Frederick Douglass, who often said, "Nothing yielded without agitation or struggle." What follows is my story which I hope you will find enlightening and enjoyable, even though I did not have an electrifying runaway slave background as the great orator Douglass.

I was born in March 1909. As most southern Blacks of that time, I was born in a segregated community on an unpaved street, just as many White kids were. I was destined to attend a segregated school, just as many White kids did. And, except for the affluent few Whites who had Black servants, neither race knew that what we most shared was poverty, common land, and similar dreams.

On rare occasions, our racial paths crossed on the town square. Kids would glance curiously and sympathetically at each other as they were tugged along by parents who pretended to be oblivious to other parents as they went their separate ways. We were neighbors, yet strangers, separated by an invisible wall imposed by Whites.

I was never told nor warned by my parents about race relations. I was never told what I might have to later learn or unlearn. Instead, pride and self-respect were instilled in me and my brother and sisters. I never missed things I did not have and what I did have seemed more than enough. I had no occasion to feel inferior because I knew nothing of what at least supposedly, constituted the superior. Later in life, I began to grasp the nature of things intuitively and upon reflection surmised that:

(1) neither superiority nor inferiority is measured by shades of color;

(2) there is efficiency and inefficiency, adequacy and inadequacy in all races; and

(3) mind and soul, not texture of skin are the standards by which mankind is ultimately measured.

Still, to rise above the narrow confines imposed by racism and the crippling influence of prejudice was nearly a lifetime assignment. Even where there is a willingness, it takes a long time to change deeply entrenched customs and traditions. Gradually, I recognized this dilemma and learned how to deal with it through patience and understanding.

I had some ideas of what I wanted to do with my life, what I expected to get out of life. Firstly, I had the good fortune to have parents who welded together a closely knit family and who inspired and motivated me and my siblings by perception and example. I didn't realize how significant and sustaining my parents' influence was until pressures on me as a "trailblazing insurance businessman" sought to restrict and limit me. As I faced problems as a minority, more than once I recalled the admonition of my mother, saying, "Keep the faith of a mustard seed, and you can move mountains."

Secondly I think it helps if we view life as a trip that begins at birth. We can discover a sense of direction our lives should take when we think, plan, and rationalize. We must have some plan for life, some dream that becomes a passion, a road map, and a time schedule that is rigorously adhered to. Until we reach a time of discernment, our future is in the hands of others, for better or for worse.

I have always enjoyed a sense of self-reliance and independence. I never wanted to be restricted or subjected to the limitations of others in the realization of my personal ambitions, which to me, were very well-defined. Believing firmly in the equity of nature, I have always believed that anything the human mind can conceive, it can achieve. Therefore, I never feared opposition or difficulties once I was sure the cause was right. I learned never to quit when my objective was delayed. Instead, I renewed my efforts with added strength.

I often repeated to myself, among other things, a part of a poem I learned in school.

> *It's easy to cry, you are beaten and die,*
> *It's easy to crawfish and crawl,*
> *But to fight and to fight and to fight when hope's out of sight,*
> *That's the best game of them all,*
> *And though you come out of each quailing bout,*
> *All broken, beaten, and scared,*
> *Just have one more try,*
> *It's so easy to die,*
> *It's the keeping on living that's hard!*

It is constant struggle that triumphs over adversity or evil. But, sometimes, instead of force, a little understanding at the right time, a bit of promoting and patience can help speed up the conquest.

In a quiet, persistent way, I tried to find the "Achilles' heel" of those who might oppose or attempt to block my progress. I found out early that a person who felt superior had to constantly remind himself of his self-acclaimed role to be reassured that his status was both valid and viable.

I thought it necessary to cultivate the "superior." One way I achieved this was to ask for advice and instructions even from those who had even lesser mental equipment. If they were potential enemies, I tried to make them my friends. I did not always succeed, but at least they were put in an awkward position if they vigorously opposed someone who only indicated he admired what his "superior" was doing. There definitely was a need to be cunning in what one wanted to accomplish.

Yet, on the whole, I always preferred to be genuine and forthright. In fact, I found it easy to make friends and I respected individuals for what they were and stood for. I had no preconceived notions that affected my relationship or respect for a person based upon race or any other classification. Along the way, I drew other general conclusions which I hope others will take under advisement.

I have always tried to avoid being involved in highly controversial issues which had no sound or constructive ultimate objective. Whenever I took a position, I tried always to defend what was good for the total community, free of my own selfish interest.

The basis for developing a strategy of survival is to create an atmosphere of truth and confidence in everything with which you are associated. What may appear to be a popular opinion or view may not necessarily be sound or valid.

While holding firmly to your principles, maintain a degree of flexibility. There are no "pat" answers to every problem you face in life. Circumstances may require a variety of approaches to arrive at the right strategy and the desired solution. Therefore, by all means, do not be afraid to be innovative and creative.

Associate yourself with worthwhile causes in the community. Be counted among those who are building a sound and durable foundation for growth, development, and improvement. Don't get caught riding a falling elevator, in other words, programs or ideas doomed for failure.

Never ask of your friends or associates anything they cannot grant with honor and self-respect. Likewise, never take a position or act in a way that reflects poorly on your character or diminishes your self-respect or credibility in your own eyes or the eyes of others.

One thing is basic: Be, in reality, all that you appear to be. Don't give the impression of being anything but yourself. That is precisely what you have got to deal with, live with, and manage for better or worse, the rest of your life. Anything else is the height of hypocrisy. Your real self in the nature of things will eventually surface.

Maintain and insist on a high degree of professional integrity and self-respect. By all means, be dependable. Let it be known, by example, that you can be relied upon to live up to any commitment you make. As the old saying goes, "Say what you mean, and mean what you say."

Respect the opinions and limitations of others, whether they are in agreement with your own or not. No one has a monopoly on what is absolute truth. It is a good sign of self-examination to pursue what you do not know, and know that others have answers to what may be questions to you.

Don't be ashamed to ask for help where you need it, no matter what you need. You can increase your knowledge and efficiency more by listening and less talking.

It is important to keep your ultimate objective clearly focused before you so that no steps are taken that are not essential to the achievement of your dreams and aspirations. Hold on to your dreams and ambitions. Do not diminish them to accommodate the limited view of others who may feel your plans and goals cannot be reached.

Finally, do not try to build the foundation to your dreams with borrowed tools. Do as David did against the evil giant. Stick to your slingshot and rocks, and leave armor and sword to Saul. Goliath is the enemy who is in your path to success and victory. Face him with the weapons you know best, those that have been tried and proven by your own skills. This I learned to do as Thurman would say, "Beyond The Timberline."

J. M. Alexander, Sr

I WILL NOT GIVE UP

"It was above the timberline. The steady march of the forest had stopped as if some invisible barrier had been erected beyond which no trees dared to be even in single file. Beyond were barren patches and strong untrammeled winds. Here and there were short tufts of evergreen bushes that had somehow managed to survive despite the severe pressures under which they had to live. They were not lush, they lacked the kind of grace of the vegetation below the timberline, but they were alive and hardy. Upon close investigation, however, it was found that these were not ordinary shrubs. The formation of the needles, etc., was identical with that of the trees farther down. As a matter of fact, they looked like branches of the other trees. When one actually examined them, the astounding revelation was that these were branches.

"For, hugging the ground, following the shape of the terrain, were trees that could not grow upright, following the pattern of their kind. Instead, they were growing as vines grow along the ground, and what seemed to be patches of stunned shrubs were rows of branches of growing, developing trees. What must have been the tortuous frustration and the stubborn battle that had finally resulted in this strange phenomenon!

"It is as if the tree had said: I am destined to reach for the skies and embrace in my arms the wind, the rain, the snow and the sun, singing my song of joy to all the heavens. But this I cannot do. I have taken root beyond the timberline, and yet I do not want to die. I must work out a method, a way of life, that will yield growth and development for me despite the contradictions under which I must eke out my days. In the end, I may not look like the other trees. I may not be what all that is within me cries out to be. But I will not give up. I will use to the full every resource in me and about me to answer life with life. In so doing, I shall affirm that this is the kind of universe that sustains, upon demand, the life that is in it.

"I wonder if I dare to act even as the tree acts.

"I wonder! I wonder! Do you?"

Howard Thurman

The Early Years

Out of the dawn of the day
A new year is borne,
The old one with its sorrow
Has faded and gone.

We know not what
With the future will be brought,
Neither can we
The hastening of time halt.

Live each passing day
So that when you've reached your goal,
You may have a well-lived life
Before God's altar to hold.

T.M. Alexander, Sr.

NOT outlined
p. 42-70
p. 241-259

The Early Years

My earliest known ancestor was Virgil Hamilton, my mother's father. He was a very proud, enterprising Black man, born well before the Civil War. I had been told that my grandfather, even as a slave, was blessed with special gifts. Some of those gifts he passed on to me. And I, in turn tried to pass them on to others.

Virgil was raised in Greenville, a little town in Cutler County in southeast Alabama. Most of that section, as all of rural Alabama at that time, was farm country. There were 435,080 Negro slaves in the state. This was almost 45 percent of the entire population. One-fourth of the nation's cotton production came from the state of Alabama; off the backs of Black slaves. Cotton was truly king.

As I said, Virgil was a slave. And as far as I have been able to find out, he took his master's family name of Hamilton. But despite being a slave, Virgil was taught to be a tradesman. He became a plasterer and regardless of the tremendous obstacles he faced, he became skilled at his trade. Virgil's ability was such that evidence of his work remained in Montgomery after nearly 100 years.

In fact, he was so good at his trade that his master figured it best to allow Virgil to work full-time as a plasterer and not as an ordinary slave. The master charged Virgil for the time he normally would have spent working in the fields and, evidently, made a profit.

This was not uncommon. A slave master who discovered that one of his slaves was unusually talented or even "gifted" by any standard, would allow the slave to sell his time or talent and pay a part of his earnings back to his master. This was called "buying your time." A smart slave could literally purchase his way out of slavery.

Blacks in America dominated the building crafts such as masonry, plastering, and carpentry for many years. My grandfather, his sons, and my father were solid evidence of this.

Practically all the ornate theaters in our town boldly displayed samples of grandpa Virgil's remarkable craftsmanship. There were two lions standing at the entrance of the early old mansions which he molded and carved, and a decorative church steeple that attests, with no obvious cracks, to both his artistry and efficiency. He did stucco and plastering work on St. John's Episcopal Church on Madison Avenue and also completed a sculpture of Weeping Mary for the same church.

It is good that these monuments remain as evidence of my grandfather's existence because I never knew him personally. I knew him only by his works and his legacy. However, his wife, Clara, my grandmother, I did know.

Virgil Hamilton met and fell in love with Clara, an olive-complexioned young woman who was the "house girl" of a large wealthy family in Montgomery. Grandpa wanted to marry Clara, but she was a slave.

Not to be denied, he set a plan in motion. He worked hard to save enough from his earnings, (after paying his master for his time,) to buy the time of his intended bride.

He succeeded, and Virgil and Clara did marry. Grandpa bought a home on Eugene Street, a narrow unpaved street where two alleys met.

Grandpa Virgil reared six children, consisting of three boys and three girls. He instilled in his children a large portion of himself. But as in all families there were triumphs and mistakes.

Homer, the oldest, followed in his father's trade and became equally proficient and well-known. Virgil, Jr., was killed as a teenager by another boy of his age in an argument. Richard, a graduate of Howard University, became an outstanding physician. He was close to my mother and was my favorite uncle. In fact, it is his middle name, Theodore, that became my first name.

Priscilla became a registered nurse. Louise eloped and married Cornelius "Bud" Wyman, barber by trade. They moved to Atlanta and he worked until his death at Herndon's Barber Shop near the corner of Marinetta and Broad. Hattie, my mother, married James Henry Alexander, a butcher. Mama was 18 years old and papa was 20 years old.

My father's parents died early and I never got a chance to know them. My father, I called him papa, did have a twin sister named Sinkie and several half sisters, but he had no brothers. He had a step father named Stevens who was a pattern maker for steel fabrications.

Papa use to say the Stevens, who were real light skinned and could have passed for White, were real mean to both him and his mother. But papa persevered. He had a sixth-grade education, yet, he learned carpentry. He did heavy construction, moved houses, worked for major banks and insurance companies, adjusted losses, and handled all repairs. He even worked on the Confederate White House, relocating it to where it now stands (just a few blocks from Dexter Avenue Baptist Church, the home of the Civil Rights Movement).

Papa parleyed his hard work into a top business, accumulated property, and retired after 40 years with better than 90 percent of his business coming from non-Black clientele. In the 1920s and 1930s, my father was probably the most successful Black contractor in Montgomery.

During his entire career in a hazardous field, he was never sued and never failed to carry out a contract. In fact, many of his contracts were made by word-of-mouth. A price was decided upon after the job was completed.

My father's reputation was known all over the state. He kept up property for individuals and the banks. Continuing in the tradition of Grandpa Virgil, my father built Old Ship Methodist Church. I cannot recall if he used an architect on this plan, but at times he did work with or without an architect. In fact, his success as a tradesman was proof of the wisdom of George Washington Carver's philosophy: The only limitations are those that you place upon yourself.

On Sunday, March 7, 1909, Dr. Dungee, a member of our family church choir, was summoned to 421 South Ripley Street. There, mama was in labor with me. The doctor's horse, however, was too slow for my prenatal impatience, and I rushed forth unattended by a physician.

When the doctor finally did arrive, my mother said I had a concerned expression on my face. (The same expression I would have throughout my life when someone was late for an appointment or when a meeting didn't start on time.) My mother would often say that I had been in a hurry ever since I was born. To that I pleaded: Guilty as charged!

Originally I was named Theodore Moses Alexander. But, eventually, the Moses was changed to Martin because of all of the fights I would get into when my classmates would tease me about my name. They would chant, "Where was Moses when the lights went out? Down in the cellar with his shirt-tail out." This would lead to a fight. When I became older, I got the name changed. The first name I kept because I admired my uncle Theodore.

Fate decreed that I should be the third child to Hattie Mable Alexander and James Henry Alexander. I had a sister, Alma, and a brother, Julius James, who preceded me. I had a sister, Bernice, who came after me. Needless to say, I had no choice in the timing of my birth. But again, fate decreed that my birth date would serve to my advantage in later years.

By the time I was in a public school in Montgomery, my mother was constantly worried about me. I frequently got into some kind of trouble with my teachers. I constantly played pranks either on the teacher or the kids in my class.

I know that I tried my mother's patience. I loved mama dearly and she loved me. She knew I needed more care and love than my older siblings. But there were times when I was just too much for one mother to handle and she would cry.

I couldn't bear to see mama cry. When she did cry, I would make all kinds of promises to behave, if she would just stop crying.

Papa, however, was less tolerant of my antics. When mama had gone her limit with me, she reluctantly turned me over to papa, which usually was a devastating experience. Papa never knew when to put that black razor strap down. After a session with papa, I usually sat tenderly for several days.

Sometimes, when papa was really angry, I made use of an arrangement with my baby sister to save me from an awful whacking, which I usually deserved. She would cry when he whipped me. That would make him stop early, because she was his favorite and he could not stand to see her yelling out, "Stop, daddy, stop!" I paid my sister afterwards. I love my sister dearly and to this day, she is still my protector.

Tuskegee remains a vivid, personal memory of my youth. My father had considerable work at Tuskegee and built a small hospital on the grounds of the Institute.

Papa would even hire some of the Tuskegee students during the summer. When we got older, my brother Julius and I assisted my father at his business. We covered roofs on the teachers' cottage.

I recall the renovation of Booker T. Washington's home, now called The Oaks, which was done around 1925, and still stands. That was just one of our renovation jobs. We also turned an old commissary building into a home economics building. We saw the famous Dr. George Washington Carver and held conversations with him.

BEYOND THE TIMBERLINE

While Dr. Carver was known for his eccentricities, my father was known for the steadiness of his working - he always had plenty of work and people came to him seeking employment. In the 1920s, laborers were getting 15 cents to 25 cents an hour, and skilled persons anywhere from 35 cents to 55 cents an hour, which were good wages for those times.

With accounts at the major supply stores, my father ran his business very professionally. Julius typed his contracts, and I kept his books and would pay the men. Julius followed in my father's footsteps, and he could operate easily on a construction site. Julius received trades training at Hampton University. My sisters were always too involved with something else to get involved with my father's business. I wasn't particularly mechanically inclined but I did learn to do a few things, like roofing and painting.

Papa did work for the city, the state, and the local bank. He also maintained the property of individuals who owned large amounts of real estate, both private and commercial. As I grew up and watched him operate, it was rare for him to ever prepare a written contract. I would hear him talk over the phone and make rough notes as he listened to his customers. As I grew up and went to high school and college, I raised questions about his methods. I distinctly remember saying on one occasion, "Papa, are you going to do these jobs without a written contract? How do you know what you are to do or exactly how much you will be paid?"

His reply was, "I know my customers. I took care of most of their parents' businesses over two generations. They know and trust me and I trust them. My word is my bond. I have never been sued nor have I ever sued anyone in my life." He told me to remember, "Always do what you promise and let your word mean something." I never forgot this or his disdain for people who bankrupted themselves to avoid paying honest debts.

Julius and I were working with him one summer during the mid-

1920s, when he was presented an opportunity to bid on a series of large construction jobs of a well-known company. He had been assured of the contract if he padded the deal in a payoff to the persons who were to decide the granting of the contract. My brother and I thought papa should consider the proposition. Since this was quite a common practice in getting big contracts, we saw nothing basically wrong in modifying his usual policy. He never talked a great deal, but I never forgot that lecture he gave us.

He began by saying, "I have never knowingly done a dishonest thing in my life, and I have never been without more work than I could do. I have never been broke or hungry and neither has my family had to suffer because of my mistakes. I am going to submit three honest bids. One will be cost-plus-a-percentage; the other, cost-plus-a-fixed-fee; and, a straight contract, and I'll take my chances." He did not get the contract.

But there were many contracts that he did get from the most surprising sources. I suppose it was the overall respectability my father had in the community that even placed papa beyond the dreaded threats the Ku Klux Klan occasionally issued to "keep Blacks in their place."

The local head of the Klan was even known to my father. Yet, when the Klan was on the prowl, some of my father's rich White friends would reassure him that nobody was going to attack him or our houses until the danger passed.

The Klan was busy during that period, and the offer was made several times. Papa never accepted it. And none of the members of Ku Klux Klan ever darkened our doorsteps with their hoods on. Perhaps they knew that many of their houses and office buildings needed work that only papa could do. Many of their businesses, families, and livelihoods depended upon papa's talents. Or, perhaps I like to think that they knew about that black razor strap he had. Either way, thanks to papa, our family was protected.

Similarly, I remember my mother would handle social slights very coolly, especially the matter of being called "Auntie." She normally would look the person in the eyes and say, "Now, which one of my brother's children are you?" This kind of thing a woman could easily do, while a man would have to be prepared to fight taking that attitude, and some did.

My mother did not get involved in the construction business. She was an expert seamstress whose steady stream of clients, mainly through referrals, created her own business.

My mother, besides being mother and seamstress, was very club and church oriented. One club to which she belonged was The Tens. This club had contests to raise money. My mother often would enter me into these contest. I usually raised the most money and thus, won the prizes. I collected a lot of donations from papa's Black and White friends. My mother was also a trustee of Hale Infirmary, a large two-story frame building which was the Black hospital. This is where the Black doctors trained and where my tonsils were extracted as a youngster.

One time, I won a Shetland pony. As a small child this was great. As the years went by, I gradually moved from a pony to an Indian pony, to a horse. In time, I became very good at riding horses, including riding bareback.

Not long after this, our family moved to another community where my father had built a larger and more modern home with a great deal of vacant land around us. The house was two stories with a large reception hall. On the second floor, papa had a little office with a roll-top desk. There were chandeliers, a mirrored door, a large back porch, and a nice kitchen with a big pantry.

Our family was close, our home was orderly and our chores were assigned and executed without question or excuses. We ate together at a specific time, and no one dared begin until the head of the house sat and blessed the table.

The Early Years

Although we were a steady church going family, we were not religious fanatics. We were trained to attended Sunday School and church and not to do manual work on the Sabbath. This was a habit I retained all my life. My father was a trustee of Dexter Avenue Baptist Church. My parents were not overly strict, but we kids knew our limitations. Respect was a way of life from which there was no deviation.

As I grew older and ventured beyond the realm of the family boundaries, I discovered another side of the Black\White world in which we lived. Our new home, as were most desirable Black communities, was close to a White section. I had to go a great distance to school and the shortest route was through this White community. This is when I began to see how vicious prejudice can be; this is when I started understanding what it meant to have dark skin.

I rode to school in the morning with my father or caught a ride with someone going to town, but I hated for afternoon to come. A group of White boys would always chase me home. They had checked the time pretty carefully. If I changed my route, there were "lookouts" on bicycles to notify the rest. I became fleet-of-foot during this early period.

Occasionally, I got scarred or dashed with mud balls. I later took to skates which increased my speed, but this proved a handicap; the pavement was rough and sometimes resulted in an untimely spill, much to my peril. This is when I learned the insulting names by which we are referred to.

There was one White woman who lived on the corner where my antagonists usually relented, who would try to shame them. They insulted her by calling her nigger lover. At this point, they always stopped chasing me and turned their attention toward hurling insults at her or throwing rocks against her house.

Usually I was good at anticipating their attacks and managed to avoid painful confrontation. One day, however, they tricked me. A group of them predetermined my moves and went ahead to block my exit. Before I could take swift evasive action, I was surrounded by the entire bunch. The same woman was there trying to shame them, but they were hell-bent on giving me the works. I shall never forget the moment this kindly woman yelled, "Put your books down and fight, little colored boy!"

While they were yelling insults at her, I was rolling up my little sleeves. I was ready to face them and then I offered to take them on, one at a time. What happened surprised me. Not a single attacker ventured forth to accept the challenge. Thus, my troubles were ended with that group.

Later, I got to know them by name and as I came through each day, some of them spoke or shared their half-ripened peaches and plums with me. We had become acquainted but only after I showed some self-respect and courage.

Undersized and underage, my "first experience in business" was selling. I began selling vegetables out of the garden from a cart. The peddling worked so well that papa had a little store built for me at the corner of Wetumpka Road and California Street. That was the dividing line between the Black and White communities. The store was six feet by eight feet, with several shelves, a rear door, and a window in front that let down to become a counter.

Papa gave me $25.00 to stock the store. I was about 11 or 12 years old then. Besides vegetables, I sold watermelons by the slice, fruit from the orchard, and soda pop. The sodas were kept in a tub, frozen by salt poured over ice. Once opened, the frozen pop would push out of the top and could be bitten off, like ice cream; this was one of my specialties. My customers loved the innovation and I made good profits.

Each day's earnings were kept under the house. I would keep all of it together and as mama used to say, at that point, it was "out of circulation." I made enough money and saved most of it until I got ready to go to Morehouse Academy High School in Atlanta.

The kids from the neighboring White section would come over to buy the sodas and the candies, and even the ice cold slices of watermelon. We developed quite a friendship, and I developed quite a little business for myself. We played together and sometimes had minor scraps over my refusal to extend "credit" on the second bottle of pop.

I know some of the kids who played with me were not permitted to go to nearby neighbors. Only if the families knew and respected each other and were respectable citizens could their children associate or even play together. Integration was by mutual desire, laws not withstanding. There had been and always would be this type of integration, law or no law, and there would always be segregation of various sorts, law or no law.

When I was age 11, not long after our move to our new house on Wetumpka Road, I urged mama to convince papa to buy a beautiful new bicycle for me at Christmas. But papa thought it was too dangerous for me to ride a bicycle the long distance to school through the streets of Montgomery, Alabama. I knew that if I begged mama and made promises to her, she would bring papa around. She did finally convince him in her own special way.

Papa, however, proved prophetic and I almost lost my life. One day, while riding my bicycle home from school, a car driven by a man reported to be a bootlegger, suddenly came speeding off the hill on Monroe Street. In the shadow of the State Capitol building, he smashed into me and my bike, and he didn't stop.

Unconscious, I was dragged nearly half a block under the car. To my greatest godsend, the accident was witnessed by an elderly white streetcar motorman named Mr. Perkins, who worked for the Montgomery Streetcar Company. He was coming home from work when he witnessed the bloody accident. Frantically, he waved and got the attention of the driver. The bootlegger stopped just long enough to pull my unconscious body and my tangled bike from under the car. Then, he sped off again.

Mr. Perkins got the name and license number of the car and held me in his arms until a local Black undertaker, Loveless Undertakers, arrived on the scene. Undertakers provided ambulance service in those days in addition to their normal duties. My name in my school books identified me, and the undertaker, a friend of the family, knew where I lived.

At home, I barely remember saying to my mother, "Don't cry!"

Dr. Dungee was sent for because I was in bad shape. Finally, Dr. Dungee arrived, examined me, and worked on my bruises. He announced there were no broken bones, and no need to operate. There was a little twist in my spine, however, which I outgrew.

But it was this poor elderly White man, a good Samaritan, who didn't leave until I was in my mother's arms and the doctor had been summoned, who was the hero of the story. Mr. Perkins gave mama his name and address, and then left. He visited me during my convalescence.

Several months passed before my case came before the courts. Mr. Perkins was the only witness. The final verdict, typical of the South's treatment of Blacks at that time, freed the speeding White bootlegger without so much as a fine.

But one positive thing did occur from this misfortune. A friendship was formed between my family and Mr. Perkins which lasted until his death. My father never hesitated to share fruit and vegetables from our garden with Mr. Perkins and his family. Even when away in Atlanta, and much later as a businessman, I would come back to visit Mr. Perkins on my trips home and bring him gifts. He would say to me, "My boy, my boy!" I think whatever racial prejudice I had, because of some of my earlier experiences, I lost after I met Mr. Perkins.

The Early Years

In less than a year following my accident, my assailant met with his own accident. His, however, was fatal. He suffered greatly prior to the relief of death.

I am glad there has never been a law which specified that one must be inhumane to one of another race or a greater law which immunes one's inhumanity to the retribution of God Almighty. There's an old saying, "The wheels of the gods may grind exceedingly slow, but they also grind exceedingly fine."

As with the case of my father's appreciation for what Mr. Perkins did for me, from this experience I learned also my father's high level of honesty and integrity in business. This reinforced my appreciation for his teachings. On one occasion we were assembled for breakfast - grits, sausage, eggs, and biscuits - a usual southern morning meal, which presented the opportunity for me to gain greater insight into the depth of my father's reliance upon honesty and integrity in business life.

At our house, no one started eating until papa was seated and asked for the blessing. Usually papa did little talking except to state the schedule of the day's assignments (which we reported on later at dinner). He gave assignments while eating, but this particular morning he had something important on his mind.

Before asking the blessing, he looked at my brother, my two sisters, and me for a long while. Mother was sitting quietly to his right, in her usual place. He broke the silence by a quick suck of his teeth which was a habit preceding his every indication of a speech to follow- sometimes a lengthy speech.

"Do any of you ever remember this table being empty? Have you ever been without the necessities of life? See those houses up on the hill and on the front street? They belong to me. Have you heard what happened to the contractor who, two years ago, got those construction jobs by padding his contract?"

"No, papa," we replied.

"Well, he took that money he made dishonestly and invested it in real estate. The Depression came, people could not keep warm nor pay their rent or other notes. They burned steps and parts of the property to keep warm. He lost all of the property and died broke. Don't you ever forget this as long as you live, in whatever you do: Anything you don't get right in this life, you won't keep long."

He drove and drove that issue home like driving a nail into a grinder. He pounded his message again and again. Finally, mama kicked him on the foot and said, "Jim, you've made your point. Let the children eat before the food gets cold."

Then, he became silent to say the blessing.

As we began to eat, mama gave her back-up statement summing up what he was trying to verbally beat into us. "Remember what your daddy said - you can't hit a straight lick with a crooked stick. Theodore, pass the biscuits up this way."

The Real World-
An Awakening

No man is more hopelessly enslaved than the man who falsely believes himself to be free.

T.M. Alexander, Sr.

There were no high schools for Blacks in Montgomery. Therefore, after I completed the eighth grade, I was sent to Atlanta to Morehouse Academy, the high school of Morehouse College. Most Black universities and colleges had "academy" departments. These academies served as conduits for high school students' entry to the colleges. Once you were accepted into the academy you were almost certain to be accepted into the college, in most circumstances.

The decision was made to send Julius to Washington D.C.'s Dunbar High School. No doubt, my uncle's graduation from Howard University, located in Washington, D.C., was partially responsible for this. One of my sisters also went to Minor Teacher's College in Washington, D.C. The decision of where to send me was easier. My mother had a friend, Mrs. Frances Reynolds, whose two sons went to Morehouse Academy. Mrs. Reynolds suggested mama send me to Morehouse. Having a sister in Atlanta, mama thought she could depend upon Aunt Louise to properly look after me. Aunt Louise's husband, Cornelius "Bud" Wyman, worked in Mr. Alonzo Herndon's barber shop. Herndon founded Atlanta Life. I practically lived near the heart of Black business in Atlanta when I went to live with Uncle Bud and Aunt Louise.

My Uncle Bud worked with Herndon at his shop on Broad Street. There were two shops Herndon owned, and they were considered two of the finest in America for Whites. Many White business clients visited the Broad Street shop, and it was from these men that Herndon learned valuable business lessons while cutting their hair.

Indeed, one of the first things I noticed about Atlanta compared with what I had been accustomed to in Montgomery was Atlanta's more progressive attitude. It had more Black business entrepreneurs than most cities.

Beyond my rather intimate introduction to Black business, upon my arrival to Atlanta I was also brought into the midst of another important institution, Friendship Baptist Church. My aunt attended Friendship Baptist Church, the most historical church in Atlanta. Atlanta University, Spelman College, and Morehouse all developed out of Friendship after the Civil War. The pastor at Friendship was Dr. E.R. Carter. He was a historian and, in 1894, wrote *The Black Side: A History of Black Atlanta.*

I was surrounded by history. I suppose this helped spark and sustain my intense interest in the Black experience from the historical perspective. I like to consider myself an amateur Black historian of sorts.

After a few years in Atlanta as a student I became very alert to the treatment of Blacks, at the time called Negroes, by Whites. I arrived in the customary manner of a Negro traveling in the South on a dirty, hot, day-coach behind the baggage car or in the rear end of it with the conductor taking the best seats for his office and the cinders flying indiscriminately through the windows and open door. I came out of the station through an ill-kept waiting room with "Colored" marked distinctly over the entrance and exit. I rode in a broken-down taxicab similarly identified, to a section of the city where Blacks lived and educational institutions struggled valiantly to invalidate their shabby environments.

I soon found where Blacks were to sit on the streetcars. I also found my way through the alleys to the colored entrance to the "buzzard roost" of the downtown White theaters. Segregation had been the only life I had known. Born in it, reared in it, and educated in it, I had not learned to resent it because at that period in my life I was unaware of its real implications. I did not realize that the things that I accepted as a normal pattern or custom were a part of a diabolical system of conditioning me in my unconscious moments to accept, without resentment, a status of inferiority and a circumscribed existence based purely on the circumstance of race. I likewise did not know that to a great degree my future education might be deliberately designed and paid for to ensure the perpetuation of a status not based upon my natural abilities, aspirations, or ambitions.

I couldn't help my marvel at the thoroughness with which this futile attempt at stagnating the mind and harnessing the spirit of the Negro was carried out. I had to learn that inherent in this pattern of racial segregation were vicious discriminations that were destined to shape my entire life.

As a thirteen year old youngster, I had the normal pursuits. I learned a bit, played hooky a bit, and met my future wife. But I suppose my most disappointing experience was at Morehouse Academy when I did not graduate "on time" with my contemporaries. This was a deep disappointment and I was very embarrassed. My mother came to Atlanta as if she was attending my graduation, and she comforted me as much as she could as I cried and watched my friends promenade.

She protected me from my father who was somewhat skeptical of what education beyond the eighth grade was supposed to produce. If he had discovered his investment had been misspent, I would probably have been denied a try at college. My mother, who had initially convinced my father to send me to Atlanta, warned me that this was the last time she would shelter me from my father. Additional incentive was given to the word "commitment" in my vocabulary.

It was the summer of 1927, following my belated graduation from Morehouse Academy high school in Atlanta, that I ventured for the first time above the Mason-Dixon Line. I went off to a tobacco farm job in Connecticut.

Despite its cold, northern climate, Connecticut was once a big tobacco producing state. Work in the tobacco fields attracted many southern Blacks, West Indians, and Puerto Ricans. The workers would turn to northern cities in the off-season for apartments, schools, social activities, and health services.

Professor Dansby at the Morehouse Academy had arranged for some of us Morehouse guys to go North to "work" tobacco. This was what my father believed I was to do that summer. But I had other intentions for going North. I wanted to finish my Morehouse Academy course work in addition to laboring in the fields, without my father knowing.

Going North reminded me of the times when some of our neighbors and relatives moved away and we were told they had gone North. There was an exodus of southern Blacks moving to the North. They left their homes for what they thought was a more promising and congenial environment, greater employment opportunities, and a better chance to educate their children.

Many left with great reluctance. Some returned frequently to visit relatives and some returned to stay. It had been difficult for them to adjust or "sing the songs of Zion in a strange land."

Conditions following World War I in the 1920s were getting

constantly worse for Blacks. There were riots, lynchings, police brutality, and injustice in the courts. Black Americans' contribution to the "war for democracy" was being repaid by the cold and ruthless hand of ingratitude. It seemed that Black children, for generations to come, were destined to attend broken down, poorly equipped schools that squatted like piles of rubbish upon the hills on the wrong side of the tracks throughout the South.

The most ridiculous example of segregation I ever witnessed was on returning home from Dallas one year after a visit with my uncle. The train I was riding stopped near a factory in Mississippi. The plant employed a large number of Blacks and Whites. It was early morning and folks were coming in to work. There were two entrances, side-by-side: one marked "Colored," the other "White."

I saw Whites and Blacks walk together toward the entrances, conversing as they went, lunch boxes in hand. At the entrance, however, they parted and entered through separate gates. They didn't even have to break conversation. Once inside the plant, they resumed their integrated positions and continued on their way. Working in the same place, doing the same kinds of things, and dedicated to a common cause were brothers in poverty and brothers in sin who were different for a few seconds and a few feet. This event seemed to be an extreme exercise in insanity.

If the North had anything to offer, it had to be better than what many Blacks experienced in the South. Hence, for me, like most youngsters who had never left the South, going North for the first time was a great experience to which I looked forward. The tobacco farm was located in East Windsor Hills, Connecticut, not far from Hartford. I expected a virtual paradise. We boarded the segregated train and headed North.

When our day-coach pulled into Washington, we changed to another train. There were no separate coaches for White and colored, and some of the White passengers changed from the segregated train to this train with us. The coaches appeared much cleaner, cooler, and more comfortable. There were no curtains drawn in the diner.

 I couldn't understand the change in the atmosphere and climate after you passed a certain imaginary line - The Manson-Dixon Line. There seemed no logic to the cessation of a drawn curtain and one coach filled with Whites and one coach filled with Blacks hooked together and drawn by a single engine, by crossing a single geographical boundary. But that was, again, segregation in one of its purest and most illogical forms.

We continued on North through Baltimore and Philadelphia and eventually to the magnificence of New York City. The bigness of New York was no less breathtaking than the congestion. For one accustomed to the "wide-open spaces," seeing green grass, tall trees, and feeling cool breezes, I felt miserably cramped and fenced in. I have never felt such utter loneliness amidst such a sea of human beings. The nine-to-one ratio of Whites to Blacks seemed even a greater differential in midtown Manhattan. Every person seemed to move unconscious of the other as though he lived in a world separate unto himself and completely oblivious even to the discordant noises arising from a thousand sources.

I considered that however damnable the imperfections of the South, at the very least there was a warmth, a consciousness, and a personal concern which persisted, although, at times, in an inconsistent manner. Yet, even in a completely homogeneous southern environment, where normally you might expect some feeling of apprehension of being lost or alone if Black, there was not the frigid aloneness and despair which so often engulfed you in the midst of impersonal urban crowds, however non-belligerent. I suppose this discernment has its effect in counteracting some of the unpleasant features which Blacks understood in the South with equally keen insight but without admiration.

While passing through New York City, some of us went into

The Real World - An Awakening

Harlem, then the mecca of the Negro in America. This huge pocket of Black people stitched to the upper end of Central Park and pinched between the Hudson and East Rivers, was as segregated a Negro community as I had ever seen.

The ratio of Whites to Blacks seemed reversed from the mid-Manhattan ratios. Yet, even though in a predominantly Black community, there still persisted that vast emptiness and cool, impersonal air. It was as if you did not exist and, if so, no one was aware that you were there.

Many of these Blacks had roots in the South, but "southern hospitality" had become insignificant for them as well. I knew this could never be home to me or my kind. I could never stand the strain of any environment, despite what advantages it offered, that would dull my consciousness and make me tough, within and without. To me, this did not appear to be a clear-cut victory or a triumph over southern discrimination and prejudices. It seemed more of an inequitable exchange between evils, a transition from property owner to tenant, from open spaces with green grass, trees, and fresh air to crowded, dingy flats stacked over a variety of shops, whose only distinguishing features were numbers.

Only the favored and fortunate few could afford to retire to the quieter suburbs at the end of the day while the great masses complacently moved from the noise and congestion of their work to the equally noisy congestion of the room or rooms they had to call home.

It is true that many persons may have left parts of the South that made Harlem a literal paradise. If so, I appreciated their attitude toward the South.

Harlem, though promoted as a mecca, was not utopia, nor is any place except when you make it so. Neither was it a "nigger heaven" despite what Carl van Vechten may have written in his book of the same name, which exalted the jazz, dance, and nightlife of Harlem.

BEYOND THE TIMBERLINE

The fact that people can change the profile of a community is the only hope we have for turning the hells of the world into heavens. I preferred to wage my battle in the hills I knew, amid the tall pines, muddy rivers, and winding roads. There, I could make a contribution of significance and be both benefactor and beneficiary. The dual position is indispensable to respectability.

I left New York enlightened, but not impressed or convinced that this type of escape was the solution to whatever ills or injustices Blacks encountered in the South. If greater opportunities were available for the development of Blacks, and if the progress of Blacks had been circumscribed in the South, there was little indication that the change was for the better. Whatever was gained in freedom was lost in initiative, and "there is no failure in the world like the failure in the presence of great opportunities." If the circumstances and conditions attending the processes of one's existence were so rigid and formalized that initiative and self-expression is destroyed, one's plight is far worse than another's whose initiative grows in strength under oppression such as in the South, as an instrument which becomes sharp on a hard stone.

Leaving New York, we found the New England countryside strangely reminiscent of the South. It was a welcomed relief and delightful contrast to the compact, crowded congestion of the metropolitan cities of the North. There were large, well-cultivated fields, rolling hills, and clear streams winding leisurely through the green forests. A sort of quiet dignity and solid security filled the air and upon the countenance of its inhabitants was an expression that these people believed that mind should control matter. This was a silent affirmation of personal adequacy and competency; a declaration of sufficiency to wring from the stubbornness of Nature with their bare hands, whatever was required to sustain them. Such strength of purpose, of body and mind, I had never seen more vividly and convincingly portrayed.

The Real World - An Awakening

New England resembled the South especially in the tobacco area at East Windsor Hills. But there were some strangely different and important aspects.

There were hundreds of students scattered over the farms of Connecticut. Groups had gone every year. Why?

There was good pay; transportation both ways was free; and, there were comfortable, congenial living conditions, and the atmosphere of home without the besetting problems.

There were few Blacks in the area in which we were located. There were, however, foreigners from practically every country and, of course, the Whites who owned and operated the farms. Many of the younger Connecticut native kids had never seen Blacks before or worked with them. They had not been taught to hate us or look upon us as inferior. For the first time, many of us had the opportunity to experience integration, and did not find it to be strange, or awkward to accept. It seemed a normal consequence; we worked side by side with equal efficiency, recreated together, ate together, and demanded respect of each other.

We sometimes fought. I remember one Black kid in our group, after an encounter with one of the White boys in which he emerged the victor, stating in relieved emotions, "Boy, I have wanted a chance to get that out of my system ever since I crossed the Manson-Dixon Line."

When we tried to shame him for what we considered an unfair advantage, he replied, "Think of the times it has been done to us at home and you dared not even defend yourself. Damn what you guys say, I feel good!"

I wondered what pent-up emotions stimulated southern Whites to make them take advantage of Blacks, traditionally his friend and helpful neighbor. Was racism a disease? Had Whites become addicted to fighting a ghost? Whatever it was, I was convinced White Southerners suffered from devastating poisons which made the conscious numb and petrified the heart.

We were welcomed to East Windsor Hills as were the many foreigners who settled there. These foreigners, many Irish, Germans, and Italians, who learned fast, had other opportunities and moved ahead in great strides to better jobs and more responsible positions. Some of them and their sons were foremen on the farms where we worked. Their womenfolk, many as "hardened" as men, would string tobacco leaves in the barns for hanging and curing. They could give birth to a child one day and the next day work in the garden. But they, too, moved up to better employment.

Year after year, there was the need for temporary labor from the South during the summer. Some of the professors from our school would go North to look out for us students and to act as foremen during the vacation season.

I was picker and puller. The tobacco basket we filled as pickers would be pulled down to the end of the row, put on a wagon, and taken back to the barn to be strung up. The hours were long, the tobacco rows longer, the days hot, and the evenings cool. After eight or ten hours of work, we were dead tired. Consequently, we did not get to the larger nearby cities often while we were on the farm. However, I did visit the town twice. The first time was to a picture show. I saw a Black on the street and he looked at me as I did at him, wondering where the other one came from and where he was headed. I did not see a single other Black person in the theater.

The next time I went with a group who had been before and knew their way around. I always wanted to try one of the nicer downtown eating places. It was a sort of novel experience, and we decided to venture into one of the "name" cafes. We were properly dressed, and fairly intelligent, so we thought. At least we were college students. We went in and selected a table near the rear, out of habit. And we waited, and waited.

No one made an effort to serve us and the place was not

overcrowded. One of the fellows decided to summon a waiter and did. The waiter pitched the menu at us and stood by for our order without saying a word. We knew we were not wanted but the law said he had to serve us, so we stayed for the hell of it.

We finished the meal, which we could not have possibly enjoyed. Then while we watched, the dishes were dropped and broken, and along with the silverware was thrown in the trash as was the custom. This could not possibly be. Had it spread this far from home, we thought to ourselves or was this one place owned by someone from our neck of the woods? This type of insult was inexcusable and almost inhuman.

We left, feeling pretty low in spirit. I would have rather seen a sign marked, "White Only." Then, I would have known not to enter.

Someone suggested that we go to a section where there were Blacks. I didn't know there was such a section, but there was. In fact, in a few minutes we were in a little community of Black businesses and residences, just as typically southern in atmosphere and character as I had seen in Georgia. It was as if, through magic, we had been transplanted again into the South, and after the experience I had just gone through, it was like an oasis in a desert.

I never returned to the city again during my stay. What I could not buy at the crossroad store or from peddlers who came by on payday, I'd asked someone to bring me from town. I had not developed a constitution strong enough to take racism in the fashion I had experienced up North. Nor did I possess a philosophy to deliberately seek out insults while I paid out of my pocket.

When our time was up in late summer, I made only the stops the trains made until I reached my native home in Alabama. I was vastly wiser and keenly aware of what I was destined to face as a Black, whether it was in the South or elsewhere. That one fact was certain and beyond the possibility of change. I would always be Black, and how I faced it was up to me.

I decided then that I would stake my claim in the South. Whatever happened, I would not run away from one evil place to only find evil in another. I believed, and with justification, that "some good can come out of Nazareth."

42-70
not Outlined

The Institution of Learning-Morehouse

Education is to know a thing, wisdom is to dignify it. Like
varnish on wood, wisdom brings out the grain.

T.M. Alexander, Sr.

The East Windsor Hills experience left me with a determination to redouble my efforts when I returned as a student at Morehouse College. When I began my first semester, I noted that great emphasis was being placed in the Social Sciences, Medicine, Fine Arts, and Education. Scholarships in these fields were available for advance study. Engineering, Industrial Sciences, and Economics were de-emphasized in the average liberal arts college and we ended up with no technical schools. Hundreds of Black students were being turned out prepared to become non-entities in a highly economic and industrialized society.

The challenge of my objectives and plans stimulated and inspired me to try to crowd 60 productive minutes into every hour of the period of preparation for the years ahead. I studied hard. However, I wasn't a bookworm. I was a perfectly normal college student who found time to sing in the Glee Club, participate in the orchestra, be a member of the Alpha Phi Alpha Fraternity, and be chairman of the Social Committee for the YMCA. I also joined the debating team.

I recall, while on the debating team, on March 27, 1930, Howard and Morehouse were opponents. On my team were Henry J. Jerkins and George Crocket, president of our team, now a Congressman from Detroit. We debated the proposition: The average high school graduate does not need a liberal arts education. I suppose I really put myself into this occasion because I was beginning to be critical of a whole slant placed upon what Blacks should study.

My sights during these years were on the contributions of non-Westerners to the world. I grew into the habit of collecting proverbs from anywhere I could find them. This was, I suppose, just a natural extension of my poetic side. I wrote poems constantly, eventually became my class poet, writing the class poem. Drawing on images from my experiences as manager of the track team, I wrote:

> *Life seems like a track meet,*
> *It is a race for place and distinction.*
> *We begin at the cradle, and place our feet on the line in*
> *infancy.*
> *Throughout the race there is a mad rush to break the tape*
> *of our uncertain goal - Success.*

Not the best example of what I could do, I suppose, but a sample of my omnivorous poetic soul. Also, during my college days I was active in my adopted church, Friendship, being President of the Young Men's Bible Class.

With the start of my junior year, an article in the newspaper back in Montgomery brought some feelings of pride to my mother and father when I was listed, along with two others, as having done well at Morehouse. The others were two seniors, Joseph R. Ross on the debating team, and Clyde Leon Reynolds, outstanding in business.

The Institution of Learning-Morehouse

In December of my senior year prior to my graduation, I had a contract for a position with National Benefit Life Insurance Company of Washington, D.C. The contract came in a letter dated March 12, 1931, to my professor J.B. Blayton, from Joseph H.B. Evans. Mr. Evans was director of the branch office of the National Benefit Life Insurance Company in Washington, D.C., a prominent Black insurance company. Terms for my employment were spelled out. I was to receive $1.50 per day in travel with a base monthly pay of $90.00 which was to increase to $100.00 after 60 days, and $115.00 in four months. Evans had lived in Atlanta and he and Blayton had such a trusting relationship that, in this same letter, he asked my professor to drive by in his new car to check on the roof of property he still owned in Atlanta. However, by March my plans were irrevocably changed. The company went into receivership and bankruptcy. Thus, I lost my first job before I reported for duty.

One failure of a Negro business, percentage-wise, was economic catastrophe. Some failures were inevitable because of lack of adequate capital and know-how. A few failed from mismanagement and dishonesty, but the ones that hurt most were those shrewdly engineered and cunningly contrived by those trusted as friends.

The outlook was not encouraging. I had spent four costly years preparing myself to face an uncertain but apparently hazardous future. I know now why so many dared not risk concentration in business and economics. Some of my classmates insured themselves by minoring in Education or Social Sciences so that if the going got tough, they might retreat to the one open door they knew existed for college trained Blacks - teaching.

There were always the schools where we could teach others to teach others, and so on. There were no barriers there but it was a retreat for those too weak to hang on or who might be cut off in spite of their strength. I had blocked all paths of retreat when I decided the direction in which I would go. I made sure I could never turn back and, though frightened as I realized the shortness of time, with trembling but determined hands, I staked it all on a "pitch and toss."

I had a stronger major in Business supported by a minor in Political Science and almost a major in English, but not one hour in Education. I disqualified myself deliberately from possibly pursuing the path of least resistance.

But 1931 was no vintage year on the economic frontiers of America, still struggling heroically trying to cope with the Great Depression. There could not have been a more inopportune time to graduate from college. I had to think straight, never be guilty of self-pity, and never commit the damnable sin of wishing I was other than what God made me.

I had firmly resolved that I would sink my roots deeply and firmly in the southern soil. I had to decide to face certain obvious problems which might well confront me almost immediately. I would certainly not have any immediate advantages over Whites by virtue of being a college graduate. In their minds, I would be regarded as "just any other Negro." If I attempted to prove myself different, I would probably be regarded as "an undesirable Negro." With these punches or rebuffs, I considered developing the technique to "roll away" from bigotry with as much dignity and poise as possible.

As I calculated the risk, there were times when I wondered if there was not some other place where the energy required for survival was less expensive or if those who left the South had probably failed to make the most of the advantages offered by their newly adopted northern environment. Maybe, I should try to make a go of it where there were at least no organized, aroused positions, deep-seated convictions, customs, and mores opposing me. I might find some place where my success would depend upon my qualifications, my abilities, and my ambitions without conflicting with laws a century old, yet still alive and operative.

As I approached participation in graduation exercises in 1931, I felt and faced the future, not without fear, and apprehension, but also with hope, faith, and courage. Somehow I knew the years ahead would justify and validate my confidence in the inevitable rebirth of freedom, democracy, and brotherhood in the land of my forefathers. The rivers of blood, sweat, and tears they had invested in its growth and development could and would pay equitable dividends to worthy recipients.

On that bright spring morning in June, I put my academic robe around me, with assurance that inside of it could well be a lamb off to the slaughter, an idealist who hoped for too much or a dreamer who might awaken to face the reality of an eternal nightmare. However, I had made my choice and I was satisfied. The danger and risk of the venture thrilled me. How else could I ever know the anguish of the vanquished or the glory of the victor?

As my name was called, designated to graduate with honors, I mounted the podium, received my sheepskin with my right hand, and gave the tassel of my mortarboard a confident switch to the left side, and went forth to my rendezvous with destiny. I had decided to live in the only place I truly knew and deeply loved - my native South.

My mother came to my graduation. I know it made her glad that I had justified her faith in me. The time I spent waiting on tables or picking tobacco, and other jobs, in addition to the long hours of study had paid off.

My father did not come. He did not think it such a big deal that I graduated. He said, "You've got nothing to do but study. You ought to graduate." My father reasoned that since he paid the bills I should not have anything to prevent me from studying.

Durham and North Carolina Mutual: A Hidden Blessing

*Sometimes, you are never so near victory as when defeated
in a worthwhile cause. Delays are not always denials.*
                                         T.M. Alexander, Sr.

After college, I wanted to spend a few weeks in my native home.
It was expected that this might be my last visit for some years to come,
and my parents were reconciled to it as a foregone conclusion.

The question was naturally put to me by my father first, who dealt
exclusively in the realm of rugged practicalities, "Now that you've
graduated from college, what exactly do you plan to do?"

When I answered that I did not know "exactly," I hurriedly
continued to say, "Whatever I do, I will use all the tools I have and
it will be somewhere in the South."

There was a mixed feeling of surprise and respect which lighted
his face, which I shall never forget. His only reply was, "It is going
to be hard; it has been hard for me."

"I know that," I replied, "but I can never win by running away
from a fight." My mother seemed less surprised. She remembered the
disappointment I had expressed four years before, after my first trip

away from the South.

She said, "Whatever you decide to do, wherever you go, have faith in yourself and put all you've got into your efforts. Work hard and pray hard."

She was, even up to the end in spite of blindness, a great morale builder. I am proud I inherited her faith and my father's practical approach to problems. I needed both in great abundance because the first job I had right out of college, I lost. National Benefit Life Insurance Company in Washington, D.C., like many other business during that period, folded.

Good fortune was with me, however. North Carolina Mutual Life Insurance in Durham, North Carolina selected me as a replacement for one of my classmates. My amended plans were to go through a training period pursuant to being employed by the company.

When the day came to leave, I had one last bit of homespun philosophy drilled into me by my father; it has guided me through all the experiences of my life. Wherever I deviated from this advice, there were disappointments.

"Remember," he said, "whatever you don't get right, you won't keep long." He also said, "When you begin to make money, take the long-range point of view; invest the first dollar wisely and you will never be broke again."

When I reached North Carolina, I saw up-close in operation, a valid, vibrant, living testimonial that the handicap of race was a myth. The myth of racial inferiority was exposed by the cold, calculating, uncompromising light of reality.

I found myself in a company that was founded by C.C. Spaulding, Dr. A.M. Moore, and Mr. J. Merrick in the midst of the segregated South. The company had proved its right to existence by sheer force of strength, character, and integrity. Its size and soundness demanded respect. Its very physical location defended any argument to the contrary. It was the most encouraging and revealing experience I had ever faced. I had neither heard of nor or seen anything comparable to it in my one venture North. It's only parallel that I knew of was in the South, at Atlanta Life.

I needed this sort of "lift" at this point in my life.

When the three of us in the group assigned to North Carolina Mutual reached Durham, we were placed in a comfortable hotel, also owned by the company. At the hotel, we were told to ask for whatever we needed, all at the company's expense. We ate well and more than adequately without a guilty conscience. We considered ourselves poised to make valuable contributions to the company.

The next morning, we reported to the office. We were guided by one of the junior officers assigned to acquaint us with the other officers and departments. The building was several stories tall and there, on the first floor was a bank, also substantially controlled by this insurance company.

All of this business was in the center of town, completely owned and operated by Blacks, in the deep, segregated, and discriminating South. Durham was a relatively new industrial town, built on the tobacco industry and thus, not accustomed to a long-time vested White elite, with its deep-dyed patronizing, plantation mentality.

As we were ushered out of the elevator onto one of the upper floors, I happened to be the last out of the elevator. As I passed an opened door to the left, I heard a soft but commanding and authoritative voice say, "Young man," and, as I looked around, I saw the copper-colored skin of a distinguished-looking, gray-haired man leaning forward across a long, neat desk in a thickly carpeted office. He smiled at me graciously and beckoned me to come in. The others had moved on, but I was literally hypnotized by the face of a man whose eyes bespoke a deep understanding of the economic empire he guarded and served.

His name was C.C. Spaulding. He was a much acclaimed figure in the Black community, locally and nationally. Some considered him the natural successor to Booker T. Washington and he was, at times, president of the National Business League which Washington had founded in 1900.

I went to Mr. Spauling as he extended his hand, and he said with a twinkle in his eyes, "Welcome to our company and our city. I'm President of the company." I would have been disappointed if he had not been. He looked the part in an impressive but modest way. "What's those keys and that pin you're wearing?" he inquired, as though he really did not know.

I was wearing my fraternity pin and two keys dangling from my new watch-chain that I purchased to go with the watch my parents gave me for graduation. It was as sort of affection not entirely unusual for a neophyte graduate from college - a sort of badge of identification, I suppose, that grows in insignificance as you replace it with more stable and meaningful indications of true intelligence.

I proudly replied, identifying each.

"You know, I like what they stand for, but I never had one myself."

For a moment, they seemed unimportant to me as I appraised the implication of his comment. I didn't realized then, but I learned later - the pins were just so much junk until the wearer makes it stand for something. I never touched them without remembering this incident, and wondered if I should ever wear them except to accelerate my efforts toward giving them value.

Mr. Spaulding took a personal interest in me for some reason and we became friends. I was later told he had indicated that he would like to keep me in the Home Office, but other plans prevailed.

One evening, at the end of the training period, we were called together. We had been through the mill of three insurance companies, North Carolina Mutual and two subsidiaries of the life company. The Boards were interlocking and were practically run by the same persons with equal efficiency and thoroughness. Hovering, over all however, like a guardian angel was the moving spirit of Mr. Spaulding, dedicated and consecrated to prove by precept and example, that mind is the standard of the man, and color is neutral.

Around a long directors' table, the three of us faced the officers of these companies and the men who had worked with us during our weeks of training. We were advised that we had done our work well and grasped the general ideas propounded with reasonable understanding.

I looked at the various officers and the men who assisted them, and noted the difference in personalities and points of view which they represented. They were an almost perfect machine, coordinating, supplementing, and giving balance for smooth operation, each part being important to the whole.

I saw the ease with which it was run by a master operator whose familiarity with its every part was only surpassed by the poise and dignity with which he exercised such complete control. There was a quality of respect his very presence demanded. He had been the right hand of the founders and considered one of the three stones upon which this unique empire had been so securely built. His silence was eloquent testimony of what he represented and was broken seldom except for his sage-like counsel so often sought.

It was announced that we all would be given an opportunity for permanent employment. Our background and scholastic training were virtually the same. The way we had absorbed the information and practical training indicated we had about the same level of intelligence and ability. There were three positions and they were undecided as to which one of us would be best fitted to either of the jobs. It presented a real problem and there was no sure way of determining at this point how to properly place us. It appeared to them that we were just about equal.

Although not apparent at the time, this proved to be the most fateful evening in my life and probably in the lives of the three of us.

Someone suggested that we "draw straws." I thought it was joke, but they were serious. We had no idea what the jobs were and we cared less. In 1931 and the beginning of the Great Depression, we were glad to be able to get any opportunity in our field. Opportunities for work were limited and being Black college graduates trying to get a toe-hold in the business world presented anything but an easy advantage to move forward.

We agreed to this unorthodox means of determining our future, realizing that the flip of a coin, the drawing of a straw or any other chance or calculated method would not lessen the risk we had already assumed. Furthermore, there had been one gamble (our race) imposed upon us from birth, and that we had survived was indicative that "fickled luck" had not entirely failed us.

I raised one question before we pulled the straws, "Are all three positions in the South?"

One of the officers asked, "Why?"

I responded, "I prefer to live and work in the South. I see greater opportunities for developing in the field of business, and the South is home to me."

The president spoke, changing the trend of the conversation, either in assent to my statement or leaving me to my personal desires. "Young men," he said seriously, "we are making an investment in you. We are taking a chance greater than one you are about to take. Whichever straws you draw, you've got a job and a contract, but do we have three men who will deliver, who will do the job we want done?"

"It may be a year, two years or more before we can answer that question or you can answer it for us," he continued, looking at first one of us, then the other, with penetrating glances bespeaking a deep insight and understanding of human character.

"There will be times when we both will feel we've made a great mistake, but with patience we will eventually know the truth."

Everyone around the table focused their eyes on him, giving mutual attention to his every word. Most of the men present had sat at one time or another in the same position as junior officers. In the presence of one whose record of achievement over adversity gave him the authority to speak, and qualified him to advise, they listened as though they were still in that position.

Spaulding began, "When I was your age, I wish I had been as fortunate as you are. I not only lacked education, but there were no opportunities for employment except as laborers, domestic servants, or personal services. You are fortunate that with the crude instruments available in the capable hands of rugged pioneers you at least have a place to begin a career in business. We have a right to expect great things from you. The foundation has been firmly and securely built."

Then, with almost prophetic sanction, he leaned over the table, looking at each of us, as if riveting his every word into our minds, "You are our hope for the future of the Negro in America. You who have been taught from the same books as they; you who have had the advantages of education; it is your responsibility and sacred obligation to earn and demand social and economic respectability for the Negro! You can do it by being thorough, efficient, and honest in all your dealings. You will have to crowd more in a square inch of your head than the other fellow. You go to bat with two strikes against you, but expect no mercy or concessions. Be competitive and make your competition effective. If you are good, if you are able to deliver, and if you've got what the other fellow wants and needs, the matter of color in inconsequential."

As Mr. Spaulding continued, he said something which became one of my guiding formulas by which to live. Others should be so guided. He said, "Be a part of your community. Don't live on it, live in it, and contribute to its growth and development. Take part in government and insist upon the right to be a full-fledged citizen. Know the people who count; work with them and they will work with you. You will earn respect if you are respectable and can be depended upon."

Then, speaking as my father would have, he emphasized to us as individuals to, "Let your word be your bond. If you make a promise, keep it, regardless of the consequences. Live up to your bargain, even if it's a bad one, and never welsh on a deal."

His voice varied from time to time, from defiance and authoritative to a soft, sometimes scarcely audible appeal. Every word, meaningful and properly placed, clinched the point with little concern for grammatical accuracy. In the dry sponges of our inadequate and untested minds, we leaned forward in uninterrupted silence, soaking up the freshness of his experiences which the years had well seasoned and preserved

"Finally, men," he summed up in fatherly fashion, "never put a price on principle. Have convictions and stand by them. Never be indecisive when you know the right decision. Never take a position you cannot defend or one that cannot stand close scrutiny. Defend what your conscience dictates to be right, honest, and just. Be confident and assured that you will eventually emerge a conqueror."

He closed with his favorite passage of scripture which was the hallmark of all his speeches: "And you shall be like a tree planted by the rivers of water, that bringeth forth his fruit in his season; your leaf also shall not wither, and whatsoever you doeth shall prosper."

It was his blessing and benediction, a climatic conclusion, a road map, a guidepost, a chart, and a compass for all the years ahead. There were no anti-climatic comments to follow. Remembering him to this day, C.C. Spaulding was a true teacher and friend. I knew he was always proud of my success when it became evident years later.

I drew the last straw. This assigned me to Atlanta to represent the Life and Fire Insurance Company. My salary was $100 per month. Finally, it looked as if things were going my way.

The Birth of Black Capitalism in Atlanta

If the foundation is sound, the superstructure will stand. But success is a continuing process. It must be constantly won, and never finally achieved.

T.M. Alexander, Sr.

Atlanta was originally settled in 1836. It was called, Terminus, because it was the proposed terminus of the Georgia Railroad, completed in 1845. In 1843, Terminus was incorporated as a town under the name of Marthasville. Two years later, its present name was adopted.

One of Atlanta's nicknames is the Gate City because of its prime location. It is on the water table of the Appalachian Mountains and the foothills of the Blue Ridge Mountains. The Atlantic Ocean is not far to the east and Atlanta lies directly in the path of any traveller going from North to South. Subsequently, growth in Atlanta has always been brisk.

During the Civil War, it was an important military center were troops were gathered and supplies distributed. This also made it a prime target for the northern armies. In 1864, it suffered extreme devastation by General William Tecumseh Sherman. But despite that attack which ultimately lead to the fall of the Confederacy, Atlanta rose up out of the ashes of war and rapidly rebuilt and regained its prominence as one of the most prosperous cities in the South.

I returned to Atlanta as a responsibly certified employee of one of the largest Black businesses in the nation. I felt my career as a businessman was off to an excellent start. Durham, North Carolina, was a profitable place for Blacks but in my mind Atlanta was a step up the ladder. Atlanta was the mecca of Black business.

Up to the turn of the 20th Century, Blacks in Atlanta and in the country were economically deprived and had only a few scattered isolated businesses of any consequence. Burial associations and various lodges, along with church organizations with charitable commitments took care of the sick, the dying, and the survivors of the dead.

Burial associations were frequently sponsored by morticians, and eventually came under the scrutiny of the State Insurance Department. This lead to regulatory requirements as to resources, combined with sound actuary practices. Some of the better associations became our first life insurance companies, concentrating on industrial insurance, with small weekly or monthly payments.

Sections of the city were divided into debits and policies were sold and collected door-to-door by agents of the various companies. These early companies grew and prospered.

Larger White companies also went into or expanded their concentration in the industrial field. Poorer families, Black and White, who could not afford the cost of ordinary insurance paid quarterly, semi-annually or annually.

One of the earliest insurance companies in Atlanta, Standard Life, was founded by a Texan named Hemon Perry. He was ambitious, aggressive, and adventurous. During the early 1920s, with limited capital and a gift for selling, he created, through stock sales, Standard Life. He also helped to organize the first Black bank, The Service

Company, which developed property and expanded decent housing in the southwest section of Atlanta for Blacks. Change began to occur when Hemon Perry made a name for himself in business.

The Gate City Drug Store and grocery stores grew out of his efforts. All of this took place in a segregated and discriminated society, even before the first Black public high school, Booker T. Washington, had its first graduating class.

In this same time period, Morehouse and Spelman colleges were both headed by White presidents. Atlanta University was headed by Whites. This was a part of the missionary concept and carpetbagger period following the War between the States.

John Hope, a Brown University graduate, became the first Black president of Morehouse, and Albert Manley, the first Black president of Spelman. Morris Brown College and Clark College, being church denominational schools, were taken over by Black presidents. All of the colleges had some mixture in faculty, and in some instances, Whites on their Trustee Boards. Families of foundations who supported these schools with their gifts frequently had representation with the Rockefeller family, and Morehouse with the American Home Mission Board or other Baptist support organizations.

Educationally and economically, there were two things that happened around this time that were uniquely related to Atlanta, which meant more to its growth and prosperity than anything else in its history, as far as Blacks were concerned. The colleges were trying to import Black scholars to teach and lead these institutions of higher learning. A.F. Herndon, who learned finance from behind a barber's chair of Atlanta Life, brought into Atlanta talented Black college people from all over the country; Howard graduates in business; the first Black C.P.A., Jesse B. Blayton from the Indian reservation in Oklahoma; Clayton R. Yates from Tuskegee, Alabama; and, Lorimer D. Milton, a Washingtonian, educated at Brown University, who received his bachelor's and master's degrees at the same time.

These men, with the assistance of others at the college and their pupils, formed the most effective triumvirate of promoters and sponsors of Black business anywhere in the country. Blayton, Yates, and Milton took over the Citizens Trust Company Bank and used it to help develop many Black businesses that could not get loans elsewhere. Both Blayton and Milton taught at Morehouse College. Blayton specialized in accounting and Milton taught money and banking, corporation and finance, and economics.

Blayton worked in The Perry Enterprises. Milton was initially employed by Dr. John Hope to teach at Morehouse. They pooled their skills along with Yates, and joined with the small business and professionals to create, upon the collapse of Hemon Perry's conglomerate, successor institutions such as Yates & Milton Drug Store chain, Mutual Federal Savings and Loan Association, Southview Cemetery Association, and many other businesses.

The early pioneers were unselfish and gave much of their time in civic and political activities, such as the YMCA, Carrie Steel Pitts Orphan' Home, and Gate City Day Nurseries, just to name a few. A strong relationship developed between the educational institutions, the business community, and the churches. All of these business leaders were church-going citizens, trustees, and all were dependent upon each other in many ways. This created a growing political power structure.

Herndon, Yates, Milton, and Blayton all belonged to the First Congregational Church. Other churches in the community gave them active financial support. In the major pulpits, I recall there was strong and forceful leadership such as Proctor and Faulkner at the Congregational Church, A.D. Williams at Ebenezer Baptist Church, Peter James Bryant at Wheat Street, and E.R. Carter at Friendship. These Black men were fearlessly outspoken, and deeply dedicated to making Atlanta a city of peace and prosperity for all its citizens. Their successors were equally dedicated and committed.

Among those most active in picking up the torch of freedom and equality for Blacks were Rev. William Holmes Borders of Wheat Street Baptist Church, Martin Luther King, Sr., Samuel Williams of Friendship Baptist Church, and W.W. Weatherspoon. All provided leadership in desegregating Atlanta and increasing Black political influence and strengthening the economic base.

Along with what Black leaders did or attempted to do to help themselves was the ever-widening compassion and determination of White leadership to do whatever was required to make Atlanta the country's greatest city.

Atlantans, in general, are possessed with a sort of haughty arrogance, determination, and drive, that move relentlessly forward in almost utter disregard to opposition or obstruction. They possess the flexibility to shift and change as the situation requires. They had the genius to accept change as long as it meant progress, whether or not it conformed to past customs and traditions.

Just after the Civil War, when the city raised itself from the ashes of Sherman's March, it sought to raise itself about the narrow confines and the crippling influences of prejudice in the interest of higher goals.

Henry Grady, at the turn of the century, attempted to lure investors to Atlanta with the cotton expositions in the 1890s. It was here that Booker T. Washington made his famous statement, "Cast down your bucket where you are," in a speech given in 1895.

Learning the Ropes

As you climb life's ladder, if the rung behind you breaks as you ascend, be glad it held until you could reach the next rung up.

T.M. Alexander, Sr.

Throughout the early 1930s, the South, like the rest of the nation faced acute and trying economic problems. The country was in the grip of The Great Depression. Hundreds of banks failed, hundreds of mills and factories closed, mortgages on farms and houses were being foreclosed in record numbers, and more than 10 million workers were unemployed.

The country and the world struggled to regain economic stability. In general, the South's struggle was aggravated to some extent by traditional racial patterns and customs which diluted its strength to deal with the major problems. A racist system administered the benefits of the numerous "alphabetical" agencies set up by President Roosevelt to ease the effects of the Depression. But the government-sponsored programs were overtly discriminatory and even in adversity, the walls of segregation and discrimination held fast. The breadlines for the poor were just as segregated as the Democratic National Party. This effectively slowed the recovery for both Blacks and Whites.

These were years which "tried men's souls." I saw long lines for food items due to rationing. The street corners where people congregated for White employers to pick them up for the few jobs available were full.

The strain of survival during the Depression consumed all the energy that could be mustered and there was little time left for struggle against deeply-rooted customs and racial inequities. However, the paternalistic instincts that some Southerners pointed to with pride, also served the interest of the Blacks during this period.

There was no such thing as political power or influence for Blacks when I began my business career in 1931. There were scattered degrees of personal influences. Certain Blacks were able to get things done through association with powerful White influence (some Whites were reputedly not too distantly related to certain Blacks). These choice "inside trades" occurred on the back streets and byways of Black dwellings, up to the mahogany panelled and deep-carpeted inner sanctums of financial institutions with a sort of hush-hush understanding. But far too often, even favored Blacks were unable to extend their special treatment to others.

In the confusion and frustration that engulfed the average Black in his struggle for survival, there was tremendous emotional strain. He worked under the most adverse circumstances and was under constant pressure on his job where unsympathetic bosses looked upon him as a piece of machinery devoid of human emotions and impervious to the impact of the things inflicted upon him. If he had any initiative, it was frequently discounted and suppressed or the credit appropriated by his White superior. He remained unnoticed, unheralded, and unhailed. He worked at skills comparable to Whites, but he was either paid less, never upgraded, and\or sometimes denied union membership. He packed his lunch each morning, rode a segregated bus to the other end of town and was denied use of the cafeteria in his place of employment.

In the evening, he returned to a segregated community where he frequently paid excessive rents for the poorest of shelter and few modern conveniences. He was constantly tired, angry, and ready to explode. His patience was short and his mood crossed. He could not blow off steam on the job no matter how he might have been wronged or imposed upon. He had to bear it or lose his job. His intestines just expanded and contracted as they twisted in silent resentment.

The intense pressure to which the Black worker was subjected and to which he succumbed, perpetrating emotional mayhem in the Black community instead of on the job resulted in numerous acts of violence. His life was treated cheaply on the job; therefore, he looked at the life of all who resembled him as being of little value. Year after year, hundreds of murders were committed by Blacks against each other throughout the South, for the most trivial reasons. There was juvenile and adult delinquency running high and wild. Homicides known and reported reached fantastic proportions while the knowledge of many never got beyond the dingy secreted confines where executed.

It is the life along "Cat Fish Row" that is best known to southern Whites. The cook, butler, chauffeur, yardman, maid, factory employee, and common laborer was the "American Negro" which most Whites knew.

Yet, the laboring Black was the selling point with which to lure industries southward. Upon his tired back and his diligent labor, the South gained economic strength at minimum cost and offered less than minimum gratitude for those gains.

Church leadership and families supplied support to individuals to lighten pressures on Blacks. Also, Coca-Cola was one of the more liberal places for which to work, along with the public utilities which were fair-minded. These led the foundation for eventual coalition between White and Black leadership. State and city governments, however, were not inclined toward providing equal opportunity.

Blacks applied their survival techniques to great advantage and capitalized on the feeling of responsibility for which White Southerners usually felt for the welfare of "their Negro citizens," a sort of moral compensation for a stricken conscience.

My personal program was long-range, full of hazards, and certain to be trying. Time was important; therefore, I had to move with speed but not without the necessary tools and adequate spiritual fortification. I had the education I planned for myself. It led me to the first chance to put it to work. Fate delivered me in the midst of my potential adversaries to convert them to my friends. It also brought me back where I made my next most important step at a time when prudent judgement would have dictated otherwise. I graduated in June, went to work in July, and had the courage to marry in August, which I never regretted.

I met my wife, Dorothy, as she attended Booker T. Washington High School. I asked her to give up her scholarship to Spelman College and marry me. I promised her that within ten years, I would give her anything she asked for. To my great pleasure, she said yes. Martin Luther King, Sr., whom I met at Morehouse, married us at Dexter Avenue Church.

I was in need of a wife because I was in need of responsibility, something which mother long ago had realized. I thought I had to have someone to help me, not push me to reach my goals. Having a family helped to discipline and encourage me to keep my resolve firm.

Starting out, we lived in a rented room on Palmetto Avenue, southwest. Eventually, my father advanced me $200 to buy a house on Ashby Grove, also in southwest. He was determined that his "boy shouldn't be renting." The $200, however, was a loan to be paid back.

From this springboard, with determination to make each day bring me closer to my objectives, I moved ahead not without fear, but with assurance despite the new problems each day would bring.

For two reasons I walked a great deal in those days. One, I wanted to save the cost of transportation. Two, I chose to avoid the penalties of segregated transportation. I walked up and down steps in office buildings to avoid riding elevators marked "colored," frequently used at will by Whites for carrying freight. The most demoralizing thing that can happen in a battle is to be tactfully maneuvered into a position where your weakness is thrown in contrast to that of the enemy's strength before the battle has begun. There is always a danger of being so overcome by the inferior status that you might unnecessarily compromise yourself without firing a shot.

This was the climate when I took my first assignment as an agent of North Carolina Mutual in Atlanta. The task was to work on an experimental basis with two related companies. This involved selling life insurance and primarily property fire insurance-mainly fire. The Bankers Fire Insurance Company was the only one owned and operated by Blacks in the country and it was a subsidiary of North Carolina Mutual. There had been others that failed after the Great Atlanta Fire in 1917 which virtually destroyed the fourth ward of northeast Atlanta, a predominately Black section. Several larger fire insurance companies were also wiped out.

There were several dilemmas that I immediately faced. This was not a time to take unnecessary chances with limited economic resources. The gaining of confidence and the selling of the safety, security, and soundness of my companies required endurance and patience. I called upon all the resources I had to face the rebuffs I faced daily as I sold insurance door-to-door.

In some instances, I scarcely got a chance to introduce myself before the door was abruptly slammed in my face. I had expected doors being closed on me, but not by hands of the same color as mine. Needless to say, this was very discouraging. But I didn't give up. I realized I had to wage a war on two fronts and with little ammunition. I had to gain acceptance by my own people and I had to overcome the "dubious" practices of White salesmen.

For many years, Blacks had been shrewdly taught to place their confidences in Whites and to look with doubt and suspicion upon their own race. This was a sad but true fact of life that hampered many Black companies. My White competitors would stress the unavoidable failures of Black business in an effort to capture the Black market. White salesmen of all kinds could enter large numbers of Black homes with little sales resistance. I could not. Ironically, the White agents would enter Black homes without the usual courtesy one would expect essential to good salesmanship.

They kept their hats on, and they addressed members of the family by their first names. Sometimes incidents of immorality arose out of the undue freedom and familiarity of White salesmen with younger Black girls whose parents frequently worked all day, a most unwarranted and undesirable form of "integration." Life insurance companies grew "fat" on industrial insurance written on Black families.

Eventually, I found little or no resistance against Black life insurance salesmen who took the scraps that Whites were too busy to consider. In general, the White insurance companies were screening their ordinary Black life insurance risks very finely. Some White companies which would accept large amounts of insurance on highly selective Black risks charged rates in excess of the manual or stepped up the insurance age of the prospect to afford a rate that would offset what they considered additional risk, based purely on race.

Black life insurance companies capitalized on these rate differentials and began to have considerable success in Ordinary life insurance placement while waging a terrific battle for the highly profitable volume of individual and sick-and-accident lines of insurance.

Being an "Ordinary" agent for North Carolina Mutual, my contacts were with Blacks of higher income brackets who were few in number. I had a measure of success among professional people, mainly acquaintances from my college days. I gained valuable experience by listening to what was said around me and taking advantage of any opportunity that crossed my path.

I worked hard because life insurance, although interesting, failed to challenge my imagination. More and more, I saw it as merely a steeping stone and sounding board to something not yet clear, but which I felt was imminent.

The basic need of making my way, through the lean years of the Depression never disturbed me as much as the need to do something creative or to make a contribution to a cause. This was probably due to my ignorance of the real danger of failure. This ignorance also was probably my greatest asset.

Whatever it was to which I was destined to dedicate my life seemed indefinite except for certain qualities. It had to offer a challenge, it had to be a useful service, and, its only limitations had to be those which I elected to place upon it. It had to be outside the beaten and over-worked paths of no resistance, a departure from what was usually expected of Blacks in their "allocated" areas of operations. I wanted a chance in the economic mainstream where Whites dominated.

Although my greatest motivation was to my own selfish ambitions, I realized there was no escape from involvement in many areas outside my immediate sphere of concern. And I found it refreshing to escape my own ambitions and be helpful to my fellow man.

I had, from my childhood learned the importance of church membership and service. All during my school life, I had been in regular attendance in Sunday School and seldom missed a Sunday. I had worked and served in various capacities, from "keeping" the door during devotion, to teaching classes. I had found time to appear in church plays and to sing in musicals or participate in any other activities of the church. It became and remains a part of my life's interest, and I encouraged others to do likewise.

I became involved with the Young Men's Christian Association. I also joined what was then called, The Atlanta Negro Chamber of Commerce which was set up to parallel the "White" Chamber of Commerce. (Our Chamber was never quite as populous as the other but we never advertised that fact and few people questioned our potency regarding Black business affairs.) I made it a point to join all worthwhile organizations where I could serve and be served.

In all, I learned a great deal which helped me in my own program and thinking. I learned, at first hand, the problems we faced as a race, both the internal confusion and external strife. I wanted to be a part of all those things that were beginning to take place, even with their inherent imperfections which are characteristic of all human efforts.

I had scarcely begun to see my own path loom before me when I found myself getting involved and deeply interested in things which not only consumed time and patience, but required more experience than I had accumulated. This lack of experience began to bother me. I found myself becoming despondent and afraid of the magnitude of my own dreams. My own ideas seemed like childish, wishful thinking against the backdrop of dire circumstances I found among my own people.

I knew this would never do and if ever I needed encouragement and hope, it was now. I needed to get in an atmosphere of progressive-minded, serious-thinking people who were so impatient with the status quo that they were determined to change it, not by compromise or concession, but by efficiency and performance.

I sought out contacts with persons who had either achieved unique positions in the community because of their work or who were headed in that direction. I formed friendships with individuals who shared my beliefs that the quality of service and not the color of skin was the important factor for success in business and had dedicated themselves to prove it. Needless to say, this group was neither numerous nor outwardly vocal, but it was present.

As a young man fresh out of college trying to feel his way, and mindful but not completely aware of the future I faced, much of what I saw and experienced was hard to understand. I had to be taught what you can never get in a classroom in college. I had to learn more about my people and why we reacted as we did and how and why we developed the peculiar skills and techniques of survival which had at least sustained us through many trying situations any people not so fortified would have succumbed.

I experienced a few more years of anxiety to fully appreciate some of the things which my immaturity rendered disgusting and inexplicable. I had since learned the importance of survival techniques, particularly those used by minority groups. Those techniques were very useful for long range planning and delayed action. They constituted a strategy which, to the casual observer or the inexperienced, was termed "gradualism" or worse "dignified Uncle Tomism."

In fact, it was "realism" that sacrifices only one element in the objective, time, which becomes subordinate to opportunity. As I observed this approach to the solution of the racial problems of the South, it had great merit if it did not become ultraconservative and inflexible in the face of natural changes in attitudes which I also observed were taking place.

I was doing two things at this time in my life which were to mean a great deal to me in the future even though I am sure I was not fully conscious of the subsequent significance of some of these experiences. Firstly, I was trying to form a base from which to work and to centralize my interest in one single thing which offered the challenge and opportunity for personal growth and development. Secondly, I was trying to equip myself with more information about the people with whom I would have to work, associate, and live.

I enjoyed people. I could never have closed myself up in a vacuum or directed all my attention to just me and my job. I had to be around and among, and I wanted to "fit." I also wanted people to understand me so that when I expressed myself, as I knew I would, I would not appear an antagonist, but rather one with honest convictions.

I was doing little more than surviving in my business activities. I had learned in short order it was going to be a hard grind, at least until I had completed my post-graduate work in the "University of Hard Knocks." But I planned five and ten-year goals with interim objectives. Frankly, my goals seemed fantastic, even to me, but, "A man's reach must exceed his grasp or what's a heaven for?"

I worked hard and long hours and lost weight which I never regained. I waited tables on weekends at one of the local exclusive clubs to supplement my small income. I frequently brought home enough delicacies to afford my wife and me an enjoyable meal on Sundays, along with a beautiful centerpiece of flowers, also courtesy of my weekend employer.

With food fairly cheap, I managed to pick up enough in tips on a good Friday and Saturday night to buy our food for the week. We really needed this extra help because I was preparing for another event in my life that was destined to make me get up or sit down and shut up. I was going to become a father. In a few months, we both hoped we would have a boy, but we would be just as happy with a girl.

I think more than anything else that the manner in which some of my early problems were solved gave me the strong faith that I had in the South. You had to experience it personally to appreciate it, to believe in it, and to stick it out.

Similarly, no one can know the thrill of parenthood until they have hovered over the cradle of their own child. Likewise, you could never know the South until you experienced being both bruised and blessed by it.

Getting Down to Business

An instrument cannot become sharp on soap rock. It is hardness that sometimes makes men invincible.

T.M. Alexander, Sr.

In Atlanta, much to my dismay, I discovered that the Bankers Fire Insurance Company, a subsidiary of North Carolina Mutual which I represented, shared occupancy with a plumbing shop. There was one roll-top desk, a typewriter clogged with dust, and a four-drawer filing cabinet. When I observed the somewhat haphazard arrangements, my first impulse was to resign immediately.

However, the representative of the Bankers Fire Insurance Company was a kind and elderly gentleman, Mr. Frank J. Wimberly, who enjoyed the respect of the community. He made his contribution and retired from government work. Unforeseen circumstances had pressed him out of retirement back into the work force. And even though his health was not good, he had done a fair job of acquainting the community with his services.

I was introduced to him as a "special representative" of the company who would assist him and work under his guidance in increasing company business while improving services to the community. But the job was much more than that. I was assigned to set up an agency that at least had the potential of being competitive.

At first, my job entailed a more careful selection of risk. I eventually had to cancel almost 50 percent of the business on the books. Bad risks were increasing the company's loss ratio to a dangerous point. Mr. Wimberly welcomed my assistance and I needed his wealth of experience and wisdom that only age could provide.

His fatherly advice was a tempering force when my impatience and over-anxiety would seem to get the best of me. I honored and respected him. He was a natural gentleman with stately qualities and justifiable pride in his own record of achievement. He had numerous acquaintances with the "right" people, but he was much too old and too tired to utilize these advantages to the development of the business. He was holding on but not moving an inch forward, which, in business, meant that you were declining.

He worked alone except for one clerk who was really his salvation in coping with the accuracy that business requires. Office space had been rented from a friend in the plumbing business who wanted to help. This was essentially, all Mr. Wimberly could afford.

One of my first moves was to get our parent company to agree to subsidize his agency and permit us to move into a more representative office. You could not expect to sell insurance from a plumbing shop. It was impossible to maintain a neat office with pipes and wrenches scattered indiscriminately about.

The company agreed. It assisted us on our promise that the acquisition of extra business would justify the expenditure. We moved to an office in a building where directly across the hall was the other life insurance company that I also represented as a special agent. This made it more convenient for me because previously there was exactly one block and three flights of stairs between my two jobs.

Improvement in the business began almost immediately. I became more and more interested in the potential of the general insurance business and less and less interested in the special work assigned to me by the life insurance field. The challenge captivated me. We were the only Black fire insurance agency in Atlanta. And except for a few agents representing our company in the state of Georgia, there were no Blacks in the South writing fire insurance.

Our company, however, did not insure automobiles and the numerous other types of risk insurance for which Blacks offered a ready-made market. It was a field outside the "allowed" area of operation for Blacks.

As I checked into this phenomenon more carefully, I saw unlimited opportunities for advancement. I talked to a number of people, White and Black, trying to get information on the possibilities of expanding our services to become a multiple line business, covering other lines of insurance besides fire and life. I gradually became tremendously interested in property and other hazard insurance.

A closer look at the competition revealed that there were a number of White agencies dealing with Black property and casualty insurance. Some of these companies also had a real estate business operating in conjunction with them. As a matter of record, most of the insurance on Black properties was carried with White agencies and our company was hardly considered "competition," if anyone considered us at all.

But it was apparent that ownership of real property among Blacks was increasing rapidly. The southern Black was a heavy purchaser of automobiles and was considered a home lover. Blacks believed firmly that they should own at least one piece of property to call home. This was a healthy situation and made for the development of a sound community of stable citizens.

Many people inherited homes and rental property. Others were beginning to acquire property, a house at a time, for future old-age security as well as current income. A few individuals had been given homes, farms, and other property by grateful White employers who had been taught to provide for their future by sound investments in real estate.

By whatever means Blacks acquired property, they could no longer be considered strictly a tenant class. Blacks were becoming landlords, and holdings were not limited to dwellings. Blacks were acquiring considerable commercial properties. With uncanny prophetic vision, we were beginning to anticipate future expansion areas of a growing city and were quietly buying acreage outside of the city to hold for future development.

Blacks followed the pattern of the majority group in the development of their communities and put great emphasis on owning a beautiful, comfortable home. They were beginning to prove to be an excellent credit risk and found little difficulty in borrowing money on a single home to occupy. However, it was not easy at first to get loans for the purchase of rental properties because Blacks were seen as getting too competitive. Blacks got around some of the White opposition by repeatedly mortgaging their own homes to buy other properties or by paying excessive interest rates to private lenders, mainly certain rich persons.

With these encouraging trends, I was convinced that if I could get in on the ground floor and develop a business paralleling this economic growth among Blacks, it might well open an entirely new field of business. The opportunity certainly possessed all the qualifications of an endeavor in which I could expand into. The Depression year of 1932 was certainly pushing me to do so.

Mr. Wimberly was getting progressively weaker. I wished that he could have been young and vigorous so that we might have had a great business adventure together. When I discussed the idea I had, he was delighted and gave me valuable contacts and sound advice. I suggested that we form a firm bearing both our names and begin to build our organization as a multiple-line agency. And, if he would hold down the office and make contacts by phone, I would "beat the bushes" for business. This would keep him off his feet and give him a chance to get much needed rest and provide me with the opportunity to test my own ideas.

I was still holding down my weekend job of waiting tables at the club. My son was born and I had new inspiration and almost unlimited energy for work. I drove myself to the limits of my capacity. If I ever grew tired, I was too enthused and fascinated over my unrealized objectives to recognize it. I had been able, through an associate, to get a White agency to accept a few selected Black risks for automobile insurance.

My White associate wrote the policies, recommended the person, and shared the commission with us. We serviced the business and put our agency seal on top of his before we delivered the contract. Most Blacks could only get liability insurance on their cars when it was financed. Almost immediately after the car was paid for, he had to provide his own insurance.

Writing automobile insurance seemed to be a good field if I could just find a company that would accept a number of Black risks. In many locations, it was hard for Blacks to purchase cars even when they had the money. Dr. Benjamin Mays told of how he grew up in his part of South Carolina where Blacks did not dare buy a car unless "big shot" Whites approved. To act otherwise was to be "uppity."

I set out to find a White insurance company that would take on Black auto insurance. I had no idea of what I would run into, but I had decided to leave no stone unturned and keep at my task until I found just one.

I used the classified section of the telephone directory. I had decided to call all of them if necessary. If this tactic failed I had planned to write the companies directly.

The first companies I called were prominently advertised. At the onset, I made the crucial mistake of identifying myself as Black. I figured that eventually they would find out. I tried to explain that I had very promising insurance needs of my clients and I would appreciate a connection whereby I could place insurance on a selected line of risk.

One agent replied, "Did you say you are a nigger?" and hung up.

Another was less rude, "Sorry, I write a few niggers but they are good boys that I know or who are recommended by my friends. I can't have no nigger agents."

Obviously my approach was wrong.

So, I change my introductory remarks. Instead of revealing my identity, I simply inquired if they had facilities for writing insurance on automobiles for Blacks. The replies and information I gathered from the answers were a great help. I learned what many Whites felt about Blacks when they thought they were talking to a fellow White. This led to many interesting conversations. There was one I never forgot.

On one call, I asked for the manager and simply announce my name which was not revealing of my race. I stated, "I am in the general insurance business and I find I have a number of Negroes applying to me for automobile insurance. I have difficulty in placing them. Could you give me any help or advice? I am just getting started and I would like to know your reaction to this type of business."

"How long have you been in business?" he inquired.

"Well, I have been doing some life insurance and a little fire business for one company, but I thought I would like to spread out a bit and go in business for myself. I just finished college about a year ago." I was glad he didn't ask which college, because I could not have pursued the conversation to its full extent.

"Wait," he said, "let me close the door."

I waited for a moment, realizing I was about to get some choice information or advice. I was nervous and frankly felt like the imposter that I was. I knew he thought I was another White man.

He came back on the line, "Listen, I had to close my door because I didn't want my office help to hear me. I would like to get in on the colored business myself, but those damn Yankee companies just won't let me write it. I have tried to tell them that there are good Negroes and bad Negroes just like good and bad White folks, but they say a Negro won't have a square deal in our courts if one had an accident with a White person. He would lose the case whether he was at fault or not. It's damn good business if you can get in on it. And they own a hell of a lot of good property, too, because I got one Negro doctor insured that's got 25 or 30 houses and don't owe a damn cent on them either."

"Well," I responded, "in a case like that what do you do about his automobile insurance? You can't tell him you can't take it because he is colored."

"Hell no! I pleaded with the company and told them he was a leading citizen and I'd vouch for him, but I had to raise his rate, and they swore that if he had one accident, they wanted the policy cancelled."

"That's a helluva situation," I replied, feeling more relaxed. "What do you think can be done about it?"

"One thing, we got to see that Negroes get a better break in court and the first insurance company that opens up to them will get a lot of good business 'cuz I would rather have some of them than some of the stuff on my books."

"Why do you say that?" I hastily asked.

"Well, a Negro knows damn well the odds against him if he happens to have an accident involving a White person, so he is more careful. And sometimes, he would rather pay a small claim out of his pocket than face those S.O.B.s' in a court. Have you ever heard how they talk to Negroes in Traffic Court. It's a damn shame."

I wanted to ask, "In Traffic Courts only?" But I made no reply.

My answers to his questions were not half as important as his to mine.

"You know," he continued, "if the Negroes get an insurance company of their own, we will lose a lot of good business because their fire business is damn good. You never hear of them burning out, and they pay their premiums on time, too. The companies writing industrial life insurance on them are getting rich. I thought once I would go into that. I once had a colored debit and I made enough out of it to go into this business."

"Well, I enjoyed talking to you," I broke in, "I will call you again sometime."

He asked, "Where are you located? Maybe I can drop in on you, or maybe we can have lunch together one day."

I got real nervous again. "I am not located yet, but I'll give you a ring. Thanks very much." I hung up too abruptly, but I was afraid I would give myself away. I knew I was up against a real problem, but oddly enough, I became more and more confident of finding solutions.

I talked over the results of my first efforts with Mr. Wimberly whose wide experience in such matters provoked only the simple comment, "Don't let it get you down. Keep trying. You'll find somebody that will help you." The old man was growing weaker by the day. He frequently was unable to get to the office. I would visit him at home and give him reports on our business and the experiences I was having. He always encouraged me even though I had a sneaking suspicion he was just trying to keep me from getting despondent. Even though he never said so, I am sure he had already tried many of the things I tried, with the same unfavorable results. Yet, he always used to say, "You're young, you've got plenty of time, so don't give up."

Feeling inspired, I had no intention of quitting. My frequent telephone inquiries, at times with my identity revealed and other times concealed, told me what to do. I had my challenge and I accepted it. I had phones hung up on me. I was insulted, sympathized with, and promised assistance that never came just to ease me off the line.

Once, I listened to a 30-minute piece of fatherly advice on why I should "be satisfied," and not try to advance too fast. I was reminded of how long it took Blacks to make the progress they had, and that if we pushed too fast, we might antagonize some of the "good White people" who were sympathetic with "good colored folk."

On one occasion, a White man came to see me. A salesman had told him about my problem, but he had a kind of "under-the-table" proposition that would attempt to conceal the racial identify of the insured, but in the event of a claim, he would disclaim knowledge that the insured was colored or say there was some mistake. I wanted no part of anything that was not above board. I courteously declined his offer.

Throughout the ordeal to expand, we had been able to get a fairly nice volume of fire insurance business. I had been putting a great deal of time in the field and had made some new and valuable contacts, and, as I was gaining confidence with each foray, Mr. Wimberly had to give up entirely for health reasons. He was nearly 80, some said older. But although weak and tired, he had remained active up to within a few weeks of his death. I missed him afterwards for months.

I needed his encouragement and I wished he could have lived to see the problem we both had faced gradually fade away and my dream, which he shared, become a reality. Having worked with Mr. Wimberly was a beneficial part of my practical education. Now, I was left on my own to continue.

There were a few things I had wanted to do that were a bit risky and which I was reluctant to try while he was alive. I was afraid he would talk me out of my plans. Firstly, I wanted to join the local agents' association.

Secondly, I wanted to cancel the insurance on the rental properties of our insured who refused to allow us to write the insurance on their principal dwelling. I felt I was being taken advantage of and getting the worst end of the risk. I thought we should complete and merit equal consideration for the better class of business.

Thirdly, I wanted to try to get lending institutions, both Black and White, to at least refer the business of their Black customers to us.

Fourthly, I wanted to do some real advertising. I felt we had operated too much undercover and depended on only the people we knew who out of friendship or sympathy gave us just enough business to get rid of us or to satisfy a sense of obligation. I could not see the business growing as it should unless we really went after it on a competitive basis. I became relentless in my efforts to become competitive in service and facilities.

The pressure was on me. I had a business to expand, a family to support, in addition to facing daily rebuffs and insults as I invaded forbidden territories and economic citadels marked, "Reserved for Whites Only."

Then, out of the blue, disaster struck.

The one company which I represented, the only Black fire insurance company in existence, decided to withdraw from Georgia and sell its business to one of the larger White insurance companies. The news crashed around me like a bombshell. I was on the verge of giving up insurance forever and finding some other type of job.

I tried to get the White company, the new owners, to do what North Carolina Mutual had been doing. But I had little success. I was told that something would be "worked out" for me in the deal which sold Bankers Fire to Equitable Fire Insurance Company. However, I didn't like the way I was "being taking care of." And even though I was in no position to be independent or to decline any reasonable offer, that is exactly what I did. I refused to cooperate in the transition of the business until I was "better" taken care of than the purchasers had intended.

I suppose the company was not getting enough business through-out the state of Georgia to justify the deposit the state required and decided to concentrate in other states where the volume was more attractive. I didn't have sufficient time to really justify the decision they made, but to my great satisfaction, their selling out proved a boon to me. I was forced to act with greater speed and determination than I would have dared otherwise.

After Mr. Wimberly had passed and the company decided to sell its business, I moved to a ground floor office in a Black owned bank. One of my former instructors, L.D. Milton, was president of the bank and another instructor Jesse B. Blayton, was vice president. They gave me a small space off the lobby usually reserved for officers' quarters which was not in use. They also loaned me some furniture until I could get on my feet and get my business established.

This is when a sense of responsibility to my family and the fear of failure became overriding determining factors. It provided the stimulation to go into business for myself in a field heretofore closed to Blacks. I wasn't exactly sure how I would do it, but I set my heart and head to the job.

I got the telephone book and started to make the rounds where I left off. This time, I thumbed through the pages to the very end of the insurance classification. I decided to start at the back and work toward the front.

There, I saw a square advertisement that read, "The Oldest Agency in Georgia." It was founded around 1800. The current owner was John Charles Whitner. This lucky or guided flip of the telephone book pages, like drawing straws at North Carolina Mutual that sent me back to Atlanta, proved to be an important incident in my life.

I called Mr. Whitner. I felt confident that for a business to have survived for so many years meant a strength of courage to accept change and to face the challenges my offer presented. I knew it was futile to try to conceal my racial identity any longer. I had heard the worst responses already and the strategy no longer appeared useful.

As I conversed with Mr. Whitner, I could tell from the slow

deliberate voice on the other end of the line that I was talking to a "southern gentleman" of the old school. I identified myself as a Black who was trying to get a business started and briefly related the experiences I had undergone in talking to other Whites over the phone, and he seemed to have thoroughly understood and sympathized with me. I was impressed with his quiet concern and interest in everything I said.

I did most of the talking because I had reached the point of desperation and I pulled out the stops on every sale angle I could think of. I don't know what convinced him but it was enough for him to give me serious consideration.

After listening and occasionally injecting a word of encouragement he replied, "We may be able to work out something to get you started. I believe you will be able to succeed if you will be patient, work hard, and follow the suggestions we give you. I will send one of the members of our firm who is a partner and a relative to talk with you tomorrow. Where are you located?"

I was so excited, I'm sure I told him at least three times in rapid succession the address of my office. When I got home I told my wife that with this opportunity, I was on my way up!

All night long, I anticipated the visit that could mean so much to me. I planned everything I would say. I wanted to sell myself, but I wanted also to be certain of not overdoing it. I decided I would listen carefully to every word and reply only to specifically directed questions until he had finished. I would remember every point that was made and deal with them one by one. My experience as a debater in college had trained me to retain and catalog points of the opposition and to deal with them in order, in rebuttal. In my business dealings, I had learned that selling requires being a good listener. You could pick up the weak points in sales resistance and frequently make the person sell themselves.

The next day in my small office with borrowed furniture, I had my appointment. It was here that in a combination of circumstances and events set me on the road to a thrilling adventure in field of business and service to my community.

It was around 10:30 a.m. in the fall of 1932 when I met John Charles Whitner in person. He came in and introduced himself with a gentle smile on his face. He was elderly, with silver gray hair, and had a rugged face that indicated exposure to the great outdoors. His simplicity and kindliness relaxed me so much that all my plans and techniques I had carefully conjured up were obviated.

"Young man," he said, "my grandfather founded my business. It is now being run by the third generation. We were the first in Georgia and we still represent some of the same companies with which we started. I haven't been in the firm long. I am a farmer, but when my father died, I came here about two years ago to take his place with the organization. I don't know a great deal about the insurance field, but what I know I will teach you and I want you to meet my cousin who is really the senior partner and who is an expert in the business.

"I can tell you this," he continued, "if you can get enough of your people to support you and you get a sufficient volume of good business, you will find our company will be glad to do business with you. My grandfather told me that after the War between the States, he was the only agent in Georgia who was willing to risk insuring Negro property, and we were the first to insure your Negro schools here in Atlanta. We write a lot of good colored business that we have had for years and we would like to have more. You can help us and I believe we can help you. All we ask is that you give us good risks and people whom you know are careful drivers, like professional and high-class business folk, and our company will take them on at the same rate as White folks.

"We want you to give us good property and we will show you how to compete by giving better service to your folks than they are getting. If you run into difficulty, we'll go with you to see your clients, and if anybody tries to block you or go to the Insurance Department to complain, let us know. We will keep you in business if you deserve to stay, even if we have to operate your office as a branch of ours."

But of course there was one small catch.

He said carefully as if he was measuring his words with a teaspoon, "Now you can't write your own policies or sign them, at least not yet, but you can put your seal on them. We will take your order by phone and mail the policy to you the same day, and we'll give you the larger part of the commission. You collect your own accounts and remit in 60 days minus your commission. We will send you a letter confirming this and if it's all right with you, we'll see how it works before we consider a formal contract."

I was thrilled and almost speechless, but I said, "Thank you so very much, sir. You don't know what this means to me, and you don't even know me."

"Oh, yes, I do," he said. "I heard about you in our Association investigation. You are better known than you think. Your telephone calls got around. We were all warned not to do any business with you by our organization or we would be put out."

"And you still make this offer?" I asked, somewhat puzzled.

"Yes, we decided to be bigger, and we believe they will all wish they had been before we are through. Go to it, and good luck! We'll see you through."

As he left, for the first time I felt real assurance and confidence in the future of my business, but the greatest satisfaction was much deeper and more significant. My faith in the possibilities of Blacks in the South was justified, for here was a Southerner born in the mountains of Georgia who had never been beyond the Mason-Dixon Line, willing to lend me a helping hand. His faith in me was so spontaneous, I could hardly believe what was happening. Yet, there was no doubt about his sincerity. I wanted to live up to his belief in me.

Fighting with the Help of Allies

There's always competition; you may not be the best, but with determination, you'll break the tape - success!
T.M. Alexander, Sr.

Gaining Mr. Whitner's association was just part of the effort to put myself on sound footing. Immediately following the sale of Bankers Fire by North Carolina Mutual to the White company, however, I was relegated to a position of sub-agent to a White agent of the purchasing company.

I continued to write life insurance for North Carolina Mutual, but this was the manner they had decided upon to "take care of me." As a matter of fact, I was to "take care" of the White insurance company. The idea was for me to keep the business intact and place all renewal policies with the new company. I was to receive a small commission for my services and exercise only such authority over the agency's business which was delegated to me. This arrangement I had to accept or give up my position entirely.

I knew in my own mind that this was a temporary concession on my part, but I was in no position to make demands and I had no other company to which to take the business. Even though I knew their purchase could not possibly include the renewals, they could only hope to retain the business which was purchased after expiration, and that depended upon the cooperation of the agent who controlled it. I had made it my business to know personally 95 percent of the clients on our books. They knew me, not the company, and wherever I placed the business would have been satisfactory to them.

I had waited patiently to reach the point where I could discontinue this subordinate position and decline doing any business with the White company unless I could do so on a direct basis. Their representative, under whom I worked, was from the "old school," and the only Blacks he had known were in domestic service and were accustomed to taking orders without question and he enjoyed giving them.

We resented each other with mutual respect under duress. He assumed I knew nothing about the insurance business and he especially disliked the fact that I understood too well and too quickly whatever he tried to teach me. He didn't realize that his instruction was too elementary. The fact that I was a college graduate was also distasteful to him. He told me once I was "too smart." When a Black is told this by his kind, it means he isn't gullible or easily made a fool of. It is intended to remind or warn him not to appear too intelligent in the presence of recognized "superiors" or not to question too closely anything he says. It's a backhand compliment because a Black person then knows he is on-target, and his knowledge of how to protect himself against a would-be exploiter has been recognized, though not admitted.

When he called on me for his monthly report in 1932, I had prepared myself for a clean break with him and all that he represented. I prepared his report with the check attached. When he arrived, prepared to give me additional instructions on what he expected of me, I cut the procedure short.

"I will not be representing your company any longer," I said proudly.

"What do you mean? You know we purchased this business and it belongs to us."

"Sure, until all the current policies have expired. After that, they belong to anyone the clients desire to renew them with."

He asked with resentment and amazement at my audacity, "What do you intend to do?"

"I'm going into business for myself and start an agency of my own so that I can write my own risks and control my own business."

"Well, what about the business on the books? Do you intend to solicit the renewals?"

"Yes, sir, I certainly do, and all the other business I can get."

"Well, you leave us no choice but to solicit it against you."

"That's your privilege, sir. We both have a file of expirations," I confidently replied.

He took his report and left, but I had already compiled the following month's business and had delivered it to the clients with full explanation. In effect, I was on the second month's business while he was soliciting the business that had already been lost to him.

After two months of work, he had not received a single renewal. Therefore, he paid me another visit. He wanted to work out a compromise and I was in a bargaining position. I had nothing to lose and everything to gain if I could get what I wanted or could make one more step toward my ultimate goal.

"Now you know we can't give you all that you want," he began. For the first time, he recognized me as a person and appeared willing to acknowledge that my attitude toward his company and him was not without merit and justification. "We have no Negro agents representing White companies in the South, and if we appointed you, all of our White agents would quit."

"Why?" I asked. "I am not soliciting White risks."

"Yes, but some of them have a lot of colored business and no competition from a colored agent."

"Do I meet the qualifications of your company, with the exception of race?" I asked bluntly.

"Yes, but that doesn't solve the problem. The local agency organization would blackball any company that appointed you."

"Do you have a proposition that you think will get us over that hurdle and give me a more equitable deal?" I was anxious to get down to the facts. I thought that if Whitner was willing to be blackballed, then likewise for these Yankees.

"I have gone over the matter with the company officials. They recognize the local problem but have no objection to you being an agent if we can work it out locally. I can get you a licence as an agent, but we can't call you our agent."

"Do I have all the privileges of an agent?"

"Yes," he said.

"Then call me anything you wish. I want the authority to write my own policies and countersign them and I want the agent's commission."

"You can have all that with one exception."

"What's that exception?"

"You have to sign my name as agent. Just write my name and yours beneath it. You can use your own seal on the policy and submit your account like all other agents of the company, but through my office. For all practical purposes, you will be a full-fledged agent, but for the records, a sub-agent to me."

I gained more out of this than was immediately apparent. It gave me additional assurance that the business I had selected was definitely on the inside of the "forbidden areas," and the wall had been cracked. This I relished. I also realized that economics is a powerful force in this whole problem of racial discrimination. The bars will always be lowered to let the dollar drop through when it is a choice between getting some or none of the pie.

This new arrangement was very satisfactory and I had little or no personal contact with my agent as sub-agent. I enjoyed all of the authority and benefits except the unimportant designation of what I actually was in relationship to the company. For security reasons, I suppose, the proper title was withheld from me. The only real loss was incurred by the company, which had to give some financial remuneration to their White representative for permitting me to sign his name and for whatever indignity his conscience might suffer by having a Black as a sub-agent. But no matter how profitable such an arrangement was, any recognition of a Black insurance agent in the South by White companies was thought hazardous to the company's (and the agent's) welfare.

Now, I was fairly well-equipped with company facilities, at least to the point that I could accommodate my clients with insurance coverage on all major risks. I had two resources to draw upon-Whitner's company and the Yankee company that bought out North Carolina Mutual. Their combined connections were almost unlimited even though I had yet to test the extent to which they would be made available to me.

Stepping out on faith, I acted as if the rug was firmly beneath my feet and there was no danger of slippage. Therefore, I began to contact major sources of business, such as banks, savings and loan associations, insurance companies, educational institutions, and other business enterprises which controlled substantial lines of all types of insurance business.

The companies I represented directly or indirectly met all requirements as to size, strength, and services offered. It was in the area of business competition that I met opposition. Nevertheless, my friends who were experts in the field had taught me new techniques in underwriting large and varied risks that were designed to give fuller protection at reduced cost. I studied the methods thoroughly and developed the skill of accurately estimating the reduction in cost, and made written proposals to my prospective clients with the promise that there would be no obligation if I could not give them better protection at a substantial reduction. My appeal was not so much based on race or such bogus notions of "help your child to get a job." My appeal was based only on my analysis of a risk and my judgement of whether or not it was worth taking.

For a while, it almost appeared that I could do no wrong. I was enjoying an interlude of freedom from anxiety and worry. My business was meeting with phenomenal success and the public was giving me good support. My White friends, who had opened the doors for me against great opposition and in the face of tremendous danger to their own well-being were completely satisfied. The results obtained more than justified their abridgement of racial taboos. The whole thing had been mutually profitable. I found myself in an extremely unique position for a Black, especially in the South.

While still young, my first year's premiums were heavily into five figures. However, to my disadvantage, I became too well-known and, therefore, a target. I had not underestimated the opposition, and this quiet, uneventful period did not induce me to relax or to become complacent. I knew full well that I was constantly under the watchful scrutiny of those who had already officially and unofficially registered resentment.

Fully aware of the tenacity of racial bigots, sometimes when active opposition was absent, this was more frightening than seeing a White-sheeted klansman on a dark wooded road. Out here in a new field alone, I felt like a sitting duck, and I was sure unseen forces were being carefully organized to "pick me off."

However, there is always more than one force at work and even though we can't see either, we sometimes feel the presence of one more than the other. The counteractive force is usually least discernible because so often we have nothing to do with its creation, its time of action, or the point at which it will strike. It's this unseen force which so often guides our destiny: *"We who have not seen thy face, by faith and faith alone embrace, believing where we cannot prove."*

I had begun to raise my sights and go after substantial lines of business even outside my immediate territory. This was not a legal violation because so long as I did not actively solicit in other cities of my state, my license permitted me to write business upon request, any place in the state.

A schoolmate of mine in a neighboring city heard of my activities and invited me to come and see his father who owned considerable property, much of it in the downtown section of Macon. He was, regardless of race, one of the heavy taxpayers and property owners of that section. As strange as it may seem today, his kind was many times duplicated throughout the South. He enjoyed the respect of the community and was highly regarded as one of the city's leading citizens. As all of his business was done locally, his many enterprises made him a substantial purchaser of goods and services from the Whites who regarded his accounts as top priority. His insurance had been handled for years by one firm and their right to it had never been challenged, hence they had never concerned themselves with whether or not he was receiving the best possible protection at minimum cost.

When I looked over his large stack of contracts and examined them, I realized immediately his agent's methods were obsolete. I figured I probably could save him at least 20 percent in cost and improve his protection 100 percent. This I was willing to guarantee, without obligation if I failed to deliver. He was reluctant at first but I was persistent in my salesmanship. I kept dwelling on the "more for less" theme. He had been a shrewd operator or how else could he have accumulated so much in this "neck of the woods" in Georgia?

He gave me two policies, for which I gave him a receipt. We worked out a proposition which reduced his cost 34 percent, gave him two contracts covering all his holdings, and a system of payment geared to be less burdensome. We recovered over-payments due to reductions in rates for which his agent had never given him credit. He was delighted over the job and agreed to accept my proposition. I was instructed to return his present policies to the agent for cancellation and immediately cover all his properties with new insurance.

This is where all hell literally broke loose and set off the spark of my worst fight for survival. Before it was over, I had wished that I had contented myself with "smaller fish," at least until I was on a more solid foundation. Now, I was in too deep to back down.

As soon as the old agent of my latest client was informed of the change to be made, a committee of White businessmen called on my new client, among them a city official and a local banker. They accosted:

"Have you lost your mind?"

"What's wrong, haven't we always treated you right?"

"Why must you take your business out of our town?"

My friend's father now realized the difficult spot he was in. He owned considerable business interests and the city officials had been cooperative in giving him "protection" and not making themselves a nuisance by having police always going in and out of his various business places where Blacks congregated in large numbers. If any trouble occurred, it was usually hushed with the minimum amount of publicity or cost to him. He was permitted to do more or less as he pleased, without interference.

But in light of his recent activity with me, they began to put pressure on him and implied they could very well be different in their attitude and make things uncomfortable for him despite his legitimate operations. He tried to explain that his son and I were good friends and went to school together and he was trying to help me get started upon his son's recommendation. He also pointed out how I had been able to save him money and improve his protection.

His agent assured him that he could do anything for him anybody else could and that he would duplicate anything I offered. Of course he could, but for years he had failed to do so. This worried the old man who had never been faced with such a problem and a decision.

He called me long distance and told me what he was up against. I tried to prevail upon him to stand his ground. I even got my friend, the President of the Bank, L.D. Milton, who knew him to come to the phone and try to help me re-sell him, but the White pressure was too great. It was a small town and news traveled fast. It was clear they would make it pretty tough for him, even to the point of failing to sell his supplies locally, refusing to accept his deposits in the bank, declining to extend him credit, and numerous other inconveniences which would throttle, if not render impossible, his business operations.

Of course, if all else failed, physical harm was not out of the question. The Congress, at this time, had not considered lynching a serious violation of anybody's civil rights, especially a Black man's civil rights.

When I fully realized the situation, I had to yield, but I hated the circumstances which made it necessary. Here was a Black man, in possession of a great deal more than most of his White neighbors, who was not free to do as he wished with his own business. He provided just about everything for the Blacks in his community, on a segregated basis, and with their blessings. The bigots benefited materially from his success but he could only enjoy success as long as he played according to their rules.

Even though I met the qualifications to render a needed and improved service to my friend in this small Georgian town, we were not free to do business with each other. He had been threatened with economic reprisals which he could not have faced and survived. His income was based on a segregated pattern, his services limited to Black patronage, but his expenditures for services were so integrated into the economy of the community that any attempt to segregate them would meet with strong and devastating opposition. From this situation there was no appeal except to the conscious and decency of his neighbors who were both benefactor and beneficiary.

We decided on an honorable retreat than to fight a battle which neither of us had a chance to win. He did, however, benefit materially by reduced cost of improved services from those who insisted he had no right or reason for changing his business.

This little event set off my own struggle for existence that left me battle scarred. Not satisfied with a clean victory, my opponents wanted to be certain there would be no repetition of such an effort on my part to transcend upon their territories or impose my services within the inner sanctums of their sphere of traditional control.

One day soon after our retreat, I had two unexpected visitors to my office. Two husky gentlemen walked right up to me before I was aware of their presence. They weighed every bit of 200 plus pounds each. One look at them was enough for me to know they were not there for a friendly visit.

"Say boy," growled one of them, "do you work for this insurance company?"

"Yes, I do," I answered trying to hide my nervousness. I looked directly at them and smiled courteously as though they were prospective clients. I extended my hand and announced my name which of course was the same as on the neon sign. They did not accept my hand.

"We want to see your father."

They had assumed that my father owned the business and I was working for him.

"I am sorry, sir, but my father is in Alabama," I answered truthfully.

"When will he be back?"

"He lives there and he won't be here soon, as far as I know."

"Well, where is the man who owns this company?"

"I am the owner, sir."

"Are you the one who came to our town and wrote the insurance for one of our colored businessmen?"

"Yes, I am the one. Are you the ones who filed charges against me with the Insurance Department?"

Surprised they answered, "Yes, but we expected to see an older man. How long have you been in this business?"

"Oh, about two years, or maybe a little more."

"Where did you come from?"

By this time they were so astonished at my youth and my courtesy, as well as the general appearance of the bank and my office, they had removed their hats and taken seats on my settee. I mustered up the nerve to sit between them which further amazed them. At the moment, it made them forget the real purpose of their visit.

Anxiously, I began to talk. And for a while, I thought I would talk them to death. I gave them a complete history of my business and the problems I had encountered. I told them I was southern-born and educated, and my ambition was to develop a business in a field heretofore untouched by Blacks. I gave them a job talk and appealed to their spirit of decency and fair play. I answered every question they asked honestly and frankly. I tried not to offend them or to insult their intelligence. They accorded me the same consideration. We talked freely for more than thirty minutes.

Then satisfied, they got up to leave, and one of them extended his hand and said frankly, "We are surprised. We did not expect to meet a person like you. We, uh, expected an older man and we thought you were probably working for somebody or being used to disrupt our business. We appreciate your courtesy and we are glad we came." Then they added slyly, "We really intended to give you hell."

I smiled, and said, "Yes, I know. I could see that when you came in. You see, it is never as bad as it seems once we get to know each other."

They left without further comment.

I went into my private office, closed the door, and sighed, shaking off the last bit of suppressed apprehension that somehow I had been able to conceal in their presence. On the other hand, I was certain that a hornet's nest had been stirred and soon other hornets would emerge to sting the invader.

Called Before the Commissioner

*Sometimes man, like a stream, may run over its banks and
cause a flood of destruction in its path, but lo there is a lie
in the land, a shape in the eternal hills that directs the wildest
streams in a peaceful path, not that it chose, but God did.*
                                        Dr. Harry E. Fosdick

The State Insurance Commissioner received showers of
uncomplimentary letters protesting my activities, especially from
those who feared my inroads in Macon. I was accused of disrupting
the peaceful relationships that had existed over the years between the
"good White people" and Blacks.

Oddly enough, one letter lauded my friend in Macon as one of the
town's leading citizens who had always done business on an honest
and upright basis and never given any trouble to the "White fold." The
letter went on to say, "And not until this nigger from up there came
down here with some high-handed, fancy ideas about saving him
money on his insurance have we had any difficulty with him. Now
he acts like he is scared to trust any of us." The letters demanded that
my license be revoked.

I received a call from the State Insurance Department to report to
the Commissioner. To say that I was afraid would be a gross
understatement. By now, I was a nervous wreck and I had no time to

understatement. By now, I was a nervous wreck and I had no time to compose myself or plan what I was going to say. I had never been in the office of this Department and I was hesitant to go alone.

I called my friend Whitner, but he was not encouraging, and did not appear surprised or concerned. He simply and quietly said, "Well, go see what they want and call me when you get back."

I felt let down and the first thing that occurred to me was that I was going to be sacrificed. I suddenly remembered that I had turned a substantial volume of good business over to the agency which they would not have, had I not secured it. If I were cut off, they could probably retain the business with an advantage since the commission would not have to be shared.

All I could see was a conspiracy or a double-cross. Then I put myself in their position and I rationalized, hopefully, that if I had done this well in one year, they obviously knew I would gain momentum as I expanded my operations to the numerous untouched sources of business which they knew were in my palms. However, I concluded, why should they care what happened to me? They had survived more than half a century without my business. I'm a threat to a well-established pattern of excluding Blacks from certain fields of operation. I had stretched this thing too far and too fast. They were under pressure and had decided it was too risky.

To my credit, I had managed to start buying a home, worked up to a used car, and had started out on a savings and life insurance program. My son was growing up and we were tremendously happy in our little home which was located in Ashby Grove in the Black neighborhood. We were already thinking about our next child as we looked toward the future. I had begun to feel reasonably safe and secure in my decision to make my future in the South. I had employed Ruth Ware, my first secretary, who was beginning to learn the office routine, which enable me to devote my time to the field. I thought I was on my way, and now to lose it all was more than I could face.

Called Before the Commissioner

As I left to keep this forced appointment, I uttered a prayer for some solution and the courage to accept whatever happened, if there was no solution. I walked into the office of Commissioner Parker. His office was not private and he was surrounded by numerous assistants and clerks.

The receptionist asked "What's your name boy?" When she realized who I was, she announced to all in the room: "Ladies and gentlemen, this is the phantom whom we have been getting so many complaints about. I thought you would want to see him." With this done, I was pointed the way to the Commissioner's desk. He was an elderly man with a kind, but firm face. He looked up and said, "Sit down. How are you this morning?"

"I don't know, sir. I can answer that better when I am ready to leave."

He paused for a moment, sucked in a breath and in a loud voice intended for his office companions to hear, yelled, "Do you know you have caused quite a disturbance in this town, and this office has been swamped with calls and letters about your activities in the insurance field?"

Intimidated, I shakily responded, "No sir, I didn't intend to disturb your office, and I did not intend to break the law."

Then, quite unexpectedly he leaned forward and whispered under his breath, "I know. You haven't broken any written law, and this department can't see why you are causing such a commotion, but you are."

This was reassuring but quickly changing to a loud authoritative bellow for all in this office to hear, Commissioner Parker then said, "I understand you are writing quite a bit of business for your people and you have taken quite a chunk of it from some of our biggest agents!"

I was beginning to catch on to his tactics. "I only solicited business from my friends and contacts to which they referred me," I replied.

"I showed them how they could save money and they gave me the business."

He would yell at me again practically damning my existence for being uppity. I would look demonstratively chastised.

Again, in a whisper, he said, "I know what you have done and you have a right to do it. They could have done the same thing, but did not because your people knew no better and they told them no better. I didn't call you up here to jump on you, but to warn you to be careful, stay within the law, serve your people honestly, and you won't have any trouble out of this department.

"You ought to be doing what you are doing and some day they will learn to accept you. You are a pioneer; pioneering is hard. We aren't accustomed to colored agents representing White companies in Georgia, but you have a right to do business like everybody else and be supported by your own folks."

The conspiratorial nature of our conversation was, in effect, undermining a way of life held sacred by most of the Whites in the room. Naturally I did not mind his conduct. Therefore, I played along with the up and down tone of our conversation.

To show his sincerity, the Commissioner whispered a little about his background to me. He said, "You know, I worked for years for a life insurance company which did a lot of business with the colored people. I had a large debit on the west side and I made a lot of money, and I also made a lot of friends among your people. I owe my success and retirement to my colored clients. It was after my retirement that I was elected to this office. I could never do anything unfair to you or to any colored person. You have my best wishes. Call on us anytime if we can be of help."

With that said, he turned to his secretary and called her by name, giving her a directive. "Write those agents who filed complaints and those who called. Tell them I have investigated the matter of this agent thoroughly and find no infraction of the law and that his activities have been found to be entirely within his rights as a citizen in the pursuit of his business. I will sign the letters."

He stood and said softly, "Good-bye, young man, and good luck!" When I reached the door, my eyes were damp with the emotions that had overcome me. That spark of decency and fair play was still alive in the hearts and souls of some Southerners in the state I had chosen to call home. For all of our imperfections, as long as this "spark of understanding" was never smothered, the South had more than just hope. It also had assurance that any problem, however serious, could be solved. Whatever our differences were, there was a leveling force that would bring us to an equitable, fair, and just reconciliation.

As Dr. Fosdick put it, "Though like a stream, we sometimes overrun our banks and become a torrential flood, destroying everything within our path, and defying all human efforts to keep us under control. Lo, there is a lie of land, a declivity in the valleys, mountains, or shape of the eternal hills that will bring the wildest stream under control and direct it in a path, not that it chose, but God did."

The pace of the opposition against me did not necessarily slacken after I saw the Commissioner. The agency's local group had already organized a meeting to be held at one of the local hotels. The purpose was to put pressure on anybody doing business with me and to carry out their previous threat to boycott those doing business with me. I had no assurance from the companies or their representatives of what position they would take at this meeting, but somehow I felt I could depend on at least John Charles Whitner.

They called the Yankee agent I had been working under and gave their ultimatum. "Either cease doing business with this 'colored boy' or get out of the organization." He got out. My friend, John Charles Whitner, who had come to my rescue and helped me to open the door originally, did not attend the meeting but sent a letter resigning from the organization and stating that his dealings with me had been highly satisfactory and entirely profitable to his organization. Neither of my companies subsequently applied again for membership with this group.

An odd situation occurred following this special effort to curtail my activities in this forbidden field for persons of my racial identity. I had a series of rather pleasant visits and calls from some of the same people who had organized themselves to put me out of business. Each one claimed that in one area or another, his organization was better equipped to help me than the ones with whom I was doing business. One went so far as to offer me an extra inducement in increased compensation for any business I was able to give them.

I wound up in a very advantageous position, and I intentionally scattered a few of my "eggs" to involve a couple of the antagonists in my hazardous venture to break through the wall that had been weakened. I remained thoroughly loyal to those who started me on the road. They had risked a great deal. Whatever their ultimate motives were or the sincerity of their interest, they represented the "bridges" that had carried me over, without whom my entire future would have been changed.

Little by little, the way was becoming clearer. Obstacles and barriers, long constructed and never forgotten, began to fall aside. I was still uncertain and concerned that stronger and more permanent barricades might still arise to replace the old battered ones. I decided on a course which would protect the gains I had been able to make. I carefully designed a program to diversify my risks and spread the "fire" that had been concentrated on me as the lone target to be "rubbed out."

Soon afterwards, I secured an assistant in my work. Aside from his small business in which he spent only a part of his time, he worked for me on a commission basis soliciting business from his friends. He did very well. I suggested to him that the field was scarcely "scratched" and if he was interested, I would assist him in making direct contacts with the companies I represented. We agreed, and the details were worked out with the companies for him to independently work on the same basis as I was working. Therefore, he became the second Black agent to enter the general insurance field in the deep South representing White companies. I continued to train more men and so did he, and each of us used our influence with our companies to expand and spread the opportunities to other Blacks whenever possible.

I also had taken another precaution to help protect my business. I drew up a sales contract with John Charles Whitner for one dollar and other valuable consideration, thus selling him my business. He had given me a contract, undated, selling it back to me for the same sum. We had decided if things came to the worst and I was unable to continue to operate independently, he would keep me in business as a branch of his own office. No one knew it except the two of us, but until we were certain the opposition had given up their fight to eliminate me, we continued to operate our business as usual with a contract for the sale of my business to him ready to be filed on the next major provocation. Luckily, this was never necessary though numerous other difficulties were encountered as my business grew and expanded.

With the strong companies I now represented, there was no risk too large for me to go after. Likewise, there were only a few types of insurance coverages I still could not write. I stepped up my advertising program and worked hard to develop good public relations for my firm within and beyond the confines of racial lines. I made friends of those who would be my enemies. I called on them to request information and help based upon their superior experiences and contacts. While I went for the big accounts, I gave personal attention to the smaller clients and single-item accounts, realizing that a diversified spread of business, as well as clients was safer than concentration in the larger and more competitive accounts controlled by one individual or an institution.

I was doing well financially, but I was not far enough along to feel assured that I might not face some set-back. This led me to keep my weekend job of waiting tables. Few knew of this among my immediate associates. I felt impelled to keep before the public my identification with the field to which I was devoting my life to the exclusion of everything else. Since waiting tables was purely an economic necessity to begin with, and still expedient in view of the chances I was taking, I saw no reason for it to be advertised.

After meeting with the Commissioner, I went after two of the largest institutional accounts controlled by Blacks in the city. I met the qualifications and my company's survey revealed that I was more than competitive in cost and coverage. The head of the business institution which was the first to turn its account over to me was contacted by his White banker, as well as his White insurance carrier. I found that when a sizeable account shifted from one company to another, it became of concern to more than the person who was directly affected, particularly where it involves the business of a Black. Ordinarily, in a free competitive system, such shifts of patronage among Whites is the usual rather than the unusual.

Black customers tended to stick close to firms with whom they had dealt with over a period of time. Even when some Blacks were shown better financial gains and other advantages, the sell was still difficult. Black customers felt secure and safe with business institutions that had served them for a long period, even going into the second and third generations. A number of Black customers told me, "I never worry about my insurance. Mr. 'So-and-So' has been handling it so long I don't care to change." This had been the answer frequently when they had inferior protection at a higher cost than necessary.

Because of the loyalty characteristic of Blacks in their business relationships with Whites, it was not unusual for Whites to become interested in any change of policy or practice in regards to a sizeable Black person's account. This situation prevailed to a larger degree, if not exclusively, in the South which, because of its segregated pattern, can more easily identify what might be a trend among Blacks. There was no time wasted in determining the cause of any appreciable change in a pattern of behavior. These were the prime factors which caused my friend, L.D. Milton, to be called and courteously questioned. He expected it and was prepared to give a forthright, honest reply to which they had no logical answer. This is what he told me he told his broker:

"Our business relationships with your organization have been entirely satisfactory, and we shall always have a friendly attitude toward you. Also, we shall not forget your kindness to us over the years. I want to assure you that in making this change I am not unmindful of the responsibility imposed upon me to be sure that I am doing the right thing. And so, you will understand I am going to tell you frankly why I have decided to make the change.

"I have a young man who is a graduate of one our colleges, as a matter of fact, a student of mine. We are trying to help him get established in the insurance field. His office is here in our building and we feel it our duty to support him, if he deserves our support and is qualified to render us satisfactory service. If we don't do it, who will? I might as well close shop and stop teaching these young fellows business if, when they have demonstrated they have the ability to succeed, I fail to give them all the help I can. For no other reason, this is why I am moving the account and there will be others who will feel as I do as we develop more agents and more business among our people. Yet, we shall always continue to do much of our business with firms like yours because it will always be necessary for us to do business with each other."

When Milton had concluded, the voice on the other end of the line was silent before there was a reply. "Let me commend you," his agent said. "I can certainly not present any adequate argument to justify my request for your business in the face of your statement. You have done what any man in your position should do, and though it has been a pleasure for us to do business with you, we respect you for your frankness and your decision to move the business for such a worthwhile cause. If we can serve you at any time or render any assistance, we shall expect you to call upon us as you would any friend."

I had already secured one school account which had been handled out of the East by a board which exercised some control over the institution. When they released the school, they had to provide their own insurance protection. I got this account "hands-down" and without opposition. It was the first time I had made in excess of one thousand dollars on a single transaction. I invested every dime of the money in my business. If I believed in my business, I felt I should put all I had in it. If not, then I should put nothing in it and get out of it.

The second institutional account was Atlanta University, which was harder to get. The Board not only had to be sold on making a change, they had to believe that the change was not disloyal. Knowing that I was qualified, I had nothing new to offer except me. However, I didn't know that University President John Hope was supporting me in a big way. Eventually, he requested that I see him.

I shall never forget our meeting in his office. The secretary escorted me in. Mr. Hope didn't turn around as he looked out across the campus from his second-story office window. "Young man," he began, "have a seat." He spoke simply and politely but appeared preoccupied with the scenery from where he stood, motionless and emotionless. His dignity, culture, and poise made me slightly uneasy in his presence. With his back turned, it was as if I was completely alone.

But as soon as I was seated in the nearest chair to his desk, he slowly walked over and took his seat behind the desk.

"How is you business going?" he began.

"Nicely, thank you. There have been some problems, but I am

beginning to see my way."

"You know you have undertaken a great responsibility in trying to open up a new field for Negroes?"

"Yes sir, I didn't realize it at first, but I do now."

"If you don't make good, its going to be quite a disappointment to a lot of people and it will be harder for the next man."

"I intend to make good, sir."

"You have got to make good, and I expect you to. I am depending on you."

"I will not let you down, Sir."

He surveyed me for a moment then said, "Now I want you to go to the office of our present agent and tell him you want to share in the insurance account of the school, and see what you can work out with him."

I was dumfounded momentarily. "You mean you want me to go and ask my competitor to share the business he has with me voluntarily?" I asked this in such a manner which I am sure revealed my inner thoughts, "What kind of a fool was my competitor supposed to be?"

Mr. Hope replied, speaking clearly his own inner thoughts. "Yes, and if you are too stubborn to follow my instructions, I have nothing more to say!" He was as indignant as I was puzzled, and that was plenty.

"But, why should he give up what he has to me?"

"I have no more to say. Good-day."

I left. I wondered what kind of fool I would appear to be when I went to the office of the man who had the business and requested him to share it with me.

Nevertheless, I immediately called for an appointment, and the next day, I was in my competitor's office.

He was courteous and appeared to be in his fifties. He had a reddish complexion, blond hair, and a condescending air. I said, "I was told to come to see you about working out an arrangement for the handling of the insurance for Atlanta University."

He responded coolly, "Yes, I understand the Board voted that we share the business. It is agreeable with me, if it's all right with you. Since the business is in effect, I will furnish you a list of the expirations and compute you half of the commission on the current policies. When it is time to rewrite them, we can get together on the distribution, etc."

"That's satisfactory with me," I replied. He took me to the files and explained them in detail, and asked if I had any suggestions. "Until I have had more time to become familiar with the line, I don't think so. I am sure, however, there is little I can do to improve the service you are rendering but I want to assume my share of responsibility in supervising the account."

"Well, there is really little to do." Then he added, "You will get your commissions."

"I appreciate you willingness to share the commissions, but I don't want a handout. I expect to earn what I get. Whatever has to be done, I expect to do my share for what I am paid."

"Okay, you will be hearing from me."

I left realizing he had been told what to do and had no other alternative unless he elected to lose the entire line on the university. The president knew I would find that out without him telling me. When I went back, I called him to let him know how things turned out.

"Well", he said, "you have, I hope, made a friend of another one of your competitors." He also stated that he was not going to hand business to me on a silver platter - I would do something on my own to get it.

I then realized that he had done more for me than giving me some good business. He had fixed it so that neither I nor my competitor could handle the business without coming in contact with each other. Mr. Hope had arranged a situation where we would have to work together or suffer the consequences. We had both accepted this deal reluctantly and with resentment for reasons best known to ourselves.

The following weekend while at my part-time job, I was accidentally assigned to my competitor's table. He did not recognize me in my white coat and without my glasses. I was not surprised and did not bother to tell him who I was even though I had recently been in his office as a fellow businessman.

That night, he spent freely, drank freely, and talked freely. The drinking kept his vision a little bleary, too, I suppose. I was in a slight dilemma. Here I was serving my competitor as a waiter by night and competing for all I was worth with him by day. I overheard him speak about me to his friends. They talked about the business he was forced to share with a Negro.

As a waiter, I performed what I considered perfect service. Indeed, I was almost omni-present for their every wish which, fortunately, was mostly liquid.

He referred to me by the name we most hate and damned the fact that he was forced into a situation that made the association necessary. I heard it all and after a while I wished I had been less attentive or a more expedient waiter.

Later that night, I realized that things are seldom all that they appear, and how economic necessity sometimes make hypocrites of us all. At last, I hung up my white coat and checked in my badge. I hoped never to pick them up again. Servant and competitor is an awkward combination to reconcile. There was no doubt in my mind that it had to be tomorrow. I would try to become the best competitor possible.

First Responsibilities of Success

Time goes on forever, and the things we do make a mark for us that either blesses or haunts us our whole life through. It takes little effort to ruin a life but a life-time to rebuild from the ruins.

T.M. Alexander, Sr.

These first years of challenge, adventure, and exploration were squeezed accordion-like into a space made shorter by speed and preoccupation. I was kept too busy to be conscious of their flight.

It was like being chased into an eminent eternity with pursuers too close to hazard a backward glance to see if it was safe to alter my speed. With me, it was more than fear of being overtaken. There were extra hurdles and obstructions in the risky race I had elected to run. One stumble, one misstep, one faulty calculation in the speed and spring before the jump, and my race was finished.

It was almost ten years of constant motion in one direction, before I could muster the nerve to look back over the trail I had blazed. It was more comforting in finding my pursuers gone than in the satisfaction of having made the distance. I was aware, as I reviewed in retrospect the road over which I had come, that all along the way someone had been kind enough to remove many a stumbling block or obstacle before I reached them. I also believe that because of the kind of marathon I was trying to run, some people secretly wanted me to win.

During the middle 1930s, I concentrated on consolidating the gains and cementing the ties and good relationships I had developed among both Blacks and Whites. For all of the intensity, the struggles had not been without rewards. I was vastly more intelligent about the overall problems and gross misconceptions and misunderstandings under which the two races diligently labored to adjust and maintain a peaceful coexistence in the South. I learned how little we understood each other and how much our feelings changed once we actually got acquainted.

It wasn't long before I realized that the Negro the Southerners "knew best" had died, and Whites had not been given the opportunity to actually know the grandchildren of the deceased. Once Southerners got to know the grandchildren, I had every reason to believe they would like him just as well, if not better. As a matter of fact, I was certain Whites would discover they had a great deal more in common with this new African-American.

I discovered that it was to my advantage to persuade my opposition to work **with** me rather than **against** me. Futhermore, I found working together was less difficult once we tried to operate on the basis of mutual respect. Constantly fighting to overcome a relentless adversary rather than trying to correct him, consumes a lot of energy and time. And even if you win, the victory must be under continuous guard.

While everything I was accomplishing and doing in business and in community affairs was gratifying, this was far less important than the attitudes which grew out of the friendly relationships that had developed in the industry toward Blacks, not only as good risks for protection, but as a vast, untapped productive power. Companies modified their policies and developed new and more progressive concepts of Blacks as an assurance risk. Blacks no longer had to shop for protection, even on automobiles. Changes of all kinds were becoming manifest, although much too slow, but there were definite wholesome trends which needed cultivating and encouraging.

By 1934, I had moved out of the lobby of the bank and had built my own building next to the bank. It was a two-story structure. I took the advice of C.C. Spaulding as I prospered and was determined to live "in" the community instead of just living "off" of the community.

In general, I was always the youngest in something or the first to do this, that, or the other. I was made a Secretary to a small savings and loan association and a member of the board of directors of our rapidly growing and solidly managed bank. The alumni of my school had elected me as Alumni Trustee of the College, which by arrangement, made me Trustee of an affiliated university.

The YMCA, with which I had long been associated, asked me to lead a membership campaign that turned out to be the biggest and most successful up to that time. I was then asked to become chairman of the Board, which I did. It was completely reorganized and while I do not claim full credit, it surged forward as never before in its history.

I became a trustee of my church and superintendent of the Sunday School. In every activity I spent myself unsparingly with almost boundless energy and enthusiasm. No matter what the job was, I developed the habit of succeeding and refused to stop short of my objective. These interests, which I deeply enjoyed, greatly benefited my business and added new friends who gave me new responsibilities.

There was so much to be done and so few willing to take the time to lend aid that I could not refuse any worthy cause that came to me. I headed every campaign of any consequence at one time or another and worked in practically all community efforts. It was my aim to set a new high in each one and succeed in it with the unusual cooperation and assistance which I was able to secure.

Naturally, I joined in the activities of the Negro Chamber of

Commerce. Our organization was concerned with all manner of items. One of our main concerns was getting Black clerks into White businesses. There was some anxiety associated with this because some thought the Black trade would move to the White stores.

Also, growing out of the Negro Chamber of Commerce was a campaign to increase voter registration. Eventually, I became permanent Secretary of the Voters League and pushed hard for registration - more and more of it. Surveys were done to assist the members of the Chamber of Commerce to assess the housing needs of Blacks. At meetings of community-wide interest, such as Lincoln Birthday celebrations, I usually was a participant. I recall one such gathering at Big Bethel. At the time, I was temporary secretary of the Civic and Political League. John Wesley Dobbs, whom I sought out as a mentor, gave the principal address, while I made a minor speech.

I found myself speaking throughout the city, especially at my old college, though I was a recent graduate. One of my topics at Morehouse was "*The Negro Youth Faces the Future,*" an educational topic. I even traveled outside of Georgia to give advice on the issue of education. However, I was concerned about the total picture. In an open letter published in the *Dallas Express*, January 8, 1935, I said:

"We realize the problems that confront us and agree we need business. However, at this point what we need most is vision to see that whatever we accomplish alone other lines will be of little value unless we are citizens who have a part in molding the civilization in which we must live, as well as make laws by which our institutions must be governed.

"If education is going to make the Negro lose sight of those important factors which are the very foundation on which to build, and fold his arms hoping that the world will slow up long enough to render him pity and mercy, then we should cease to educate the youth of the Race, because its end is contradicting to its purposes and has a degenerating effect.

"May God help us to wake up to the realization that our destiny lies within our own hands, and success is just another name for ambition. In the words of the scripture: *He helps those who help themselves.*"

All in all, my involvement was focused on youth a good deal of the time. At one point, I was on the Advisory Committee of a Boys Club associated with the Law and Order League of America. But, I suppose my greatest commitment to youth was fulfilled as I became deeply involved with the YMCA. My first years of involvement with the Butler Street YMCA were exciting. Every year, goals were more than exceeded. My success with the YMCA was just as widespread as the business achievements I was making. On a visit to Dallas to see my uncle, Dr. R.T. Hamilton, a newspaper reporter was just as interested in the 1,000 new members and $5,600 in cash we had brought to the YMCA, as of my business success.

Similarly, my involvement with the Community Chest was also important and rather intense. C.C. Spaulding's admonition about living "in" and not "off" the community, involved strenuous work and many headaches. But I occasionally did something special to keep a good balance.

In September 1935, accompanying several of my older companions, really mentors I chose for myself, we went to New York to see Joe Louis fight in Yankee Stadium. We also saw NBC studios, Radio City Hall, and the Metropolitan Museum of Fine Arts. Naturally, we also took in such places as Small's Paradise, the Apollo, and the famed Cotton Club.

I suppose it was after seeing some of the night life in New York that a group of us opened our club in Atlanta called Top Hat. We competed with the activities and social affairs held on the roof of the Odd Fellows Hall, a popular place in Atlanta for Blacks to hold affairs. In general, as a Mason, Shriner, and fraternity brother of the Alphas, my business and pleasure were mixed a lot of times.

Of course, with such sustained contributions to the community, there were occasions when several banquets or Man of the Year awards came my way. One of the more prominent reasons for my community achievement awards was the effort I had put in the Butler Street YMCA. As Chairman for ten years, I had increased the budget from $12,000 to $118,000 and had been directly and keenly involved in erecting a new building worth $100,000 in 1950. An article reporting on one of the affairs honoring me in 1953, accurately states my attitude in life. It stated the following:

"His greatest joy is helping and working with people. He prides himself on helping scores of young men and women get ahead in the business world who formerly worked in his companies."

I still find it compulsive to do the same. What had happened to me was being duplicated in many cities in the South in one way or the other; not necessarily in new fields of endeavor, but scattered throughout all the areas of common interest and concern.

In 1941, the Second World War and a general feeling of unrest caused by its outbreak was a grave concern for all who loved peace. Every mother who had a son had her equitable share of sleepless nights and anxious days. War was too eminent for needless hate and groundless fears. Difficulties and common problems have a tendency to bring about a feeling of unity and kinship. Minorities have made their greatest progress just prior to, in the midst of, or immediately following periods of national disturbances or catastrophes.

This was such a period and the moral climate was right for the changes appearing in the South, although undramatic yet positive, and with little or no external stimulation. I suppose it was as a result of my general reflection on the potentially violent movements across the world that lead me to give the speech I did in 1938, *Education for Citizenship*. I began with a poem:

Rise, for the day is passing,
And you lie dreaming on,
The others have buckled their armours
And forth to fight have gone.
A place in the ranks awaits you,
Each man has a part to play.
The past and future are nothing,
In face of our stern today.

Rise, for the day is passing,
The sound you scarcely hear
Is the enemy marching to battle-
Arise, the foe is here!
Stay not to sharpen your weapons
Or the hour to strike will pass.

In my business career, I had my greatest period of expansion with more cooperation than opposition. My most loyal supporters were some of those who fought hardest to keep me from ever getting started. They assisted me in establishing several branches in another state and took out the interference before I reached it. I realized the extent of my responsibility to justify myself to those who dared to go "all-out" in my behalf. I knew that I was under constant scrutiny, and no mistakes could be made at this point.

This was not a strange position for me. I had become so accustomed to working under pressure that it was almost uncomfortable when it relaxed. There was always the fear it might have gone "underground," only to reappear more vicious and violent than before.

I tried to stay in a position where every proposition was as advantageous to those I dealt with as to me. I wanted to avoid, if possible, special considerations or concessions. At some point, we had to graduate from dependence into independence; yet, there were times when both were indispensable. The more of our own "freight" we could bear, the more we had to until we were carrying it all. It was at this point that equality became a reality rather than a sentiment.

I had every reason to believe it possible to move the same pattern I had devised in solving my personal problems into other areas of racial cooperation and good will. The assistance with the difficulties and adversaries confronting me helped me to realize that the solution to improving race relations was the dispelling of fear, creating confidence and trust among each other, and getting to know just what kind of neighbors we actually were. What Whites and Blacks really knew about each other was almost legendary and both had lived with fear and distrust kept alive by propagandizing political demagogues. Behind the smoke screens of racial bigotry, hate, and fear, irreparable damage had been done to retard the progress of the South in every area of interest and significance.

We had numerous requests from Blacks throughout the country for information and even advice on how change had been accomplished in Atlanta and what steps should be taken to obtain the same results in their communities. I questioned whether or not we had accidentally evolved anything that might be constructed to be a pattern or formula for others to adopt. How does one know when he is competent to advise others? Certainly one man who makes the distance with all of the assistance and unusual circumstances that attended my venture cannot claim superior know-how.

I was reluctant to accept the role of "pioneer," with all its implications that were being placed upon me. Yet, I had a deep concern for those who shared the same apprehensions and fears that I originally had. I wanted to be helpful if I could and, most of all, I had grown to believe that as Black Americans, we had not taken the time to explore the "myth" about ourselves, common in the thinking of most southern Whites. We had accepted a status delegated to us largely because we had never challenged it. If we were to gain the opportunities we deserved and were qualified for, we could not wait for those who had what we needed to discover us in their new light. We had to make ourselves known, felt, and wanted.

I felt that accomplishing this, was not an impossible undertaking. There were many White Southerners as new in their thinking and as willing to cooperate in bringing about a New South as there were Black Southerners wanting to be New Black Southerners.

All over the South, there were indications of this yearning for equity in race relations. We stood back, each on his side of the line, waiting for the other to make a friendly gesture or move in his direction. Interracial cooperative movements had been in existence since after the First World War. This was probably because of the explosive race riots that occurred as Blacks quickened their pace for full civil rights from the founding of the NAACP in 1908. Also, many Blacks simply refused to go back to their "place" now that the "war to make the world safe for democracy" had achieved democracy in Europe. Even in Atlanta, where the Commission on Interracial Cooperation had its headquarters, activity was abundant with promoting interracial harmony.

I became an enthusiastic promoter of the South for Black Americans. I debunked at every opportunity the idea that Blacks in the South could not advance to the maximum of their capacities, not without hindrance, but with aid and assistance . The advances made in the South, and especially Atlanta, were testimonial to that fact. Nowhere had people with so little advanced this far in as short a period of time.

If segregation had been a barrier to Blacks, we converted it into the greatest boost of all ages. If we were crowded and cramped, we multiplied out of our confinement, bigger, stronger, and more powerful because of it. When we found the doors closed against us, we made new openings that could not be closed.

My optimism and enthusiasm for the South were well known. I could talk about my feelings with authority. I had experienced the things of which I spoke. I had stayed in the South, determined to help build and protect it; and yes, change it where it needed changing, and there were plenty of areas in which to work. I had dared to believe in it and I had not run away. I believed that it was my responsibility to keep my home fit to live in and worthy to die for.

In 1939, while in New York, I attended a meeting of my national fraternity, Alpha Phi Alpha. The meetings were held on the campus of one of the universities. Members came from all over the country. Speakers outlined their problems and what they had attempted to do to solve them. One brother told of the efforts to get Black drivers on dairy trucks in Black communities. He was pleased to report success after a boycott of the dairy's product by Blacks.

Toward the end of his speech, he bemoaned the plight of the brothers in the South and the need for the organization to give leadership and help to its southern members. One speaker after another, none living in the South, talked about things he had heard and read. They made a strong appeal for those of us unfortunate enough to live below the Mason-Dixon Line.

I was not listed on the program. I was not even a delegate. I was on a vacation and decided I would attend the meeting. But I had taken about as much as I could. I got the attention of the presiding officer who immediately invited me forward. Everyone supposed I was expected to validate what had been said and enumerate a few more of our "problems in the South."

"Mr. Chairman and brothers," I began, "I believe I have the right to speak to the points made by the last few speakers. I am a native Southerner, and I have never been away from the South over sixty days. I know you are sincere in your concern for all the members of this organization and the

Negroes, in particular. I share your concern and your interest. I want to extend my sympathy to all of you with the problems you have encountered in your respective communities. We all have problems, and as long as we are human we'll have human imperfections which create problems. We, too, will have to, for all our imperfections, find solutions to them. When we do, we should be sure we are better off with the solution than we were with the problems. Sometimes it's adversity that makes men invincible. An instrument often becomes most keen on hard stones.

"To the brother in the mid-West, we have no Negroes driving White dairy trucks either. Our answer was not boycott. We have a Negro who bought out a White dairy and a herd of cows. He put in a pasteurizing plant, bought a fleet of trucks, and today delivers milk all over our city to Negro homes and Negro public and private schools. The small White dairy could not meet the competition of big dairies and sold at a sacrifice. The Negro dairy owner had to depend entirely on a segregated market, but he knew if he was competitive, he could capture most of it, and did. I recommend that procedure in your city in lieu of a few menial truck driving jobs.

"I noticed since being in New York this time that a bank once managed by Negroes but owned by a monied interest in New York is now closed. I understand, and my information on this is much like yours about the South, unauthoritative, that there wasn't enough Negro community support in this area to justify it. I assume, therefore, that the numerous businesses I see around are 'fronted,' and not owned by Negroes. In contrast, we have in the deep South, several Negro-owned banks. In my city, they put a Negro window at one White bank and ours doubled in size almost overnight, and now enjoys considerable White patronage. Segregated, maybe, but progressing in spite of it or because of it!

"In my own field there is not one of us in the City of New York representing a single insurance company, nor can you issue a contract and sign it. Most of the companies I represent are here, not in the South. The president of one company told me yesterday that no Negro had ever requested representation of his company and, to his knowledge, no other company. Do you own property up here where you are so free or are you tenants? I have Negro clients who own up to a hundred separate dwellings.

"Gentlemen, you provoked me to this, but before you condemn, come and see. It is you who stand in the need of help and we, in the South, offer you at least one or two answers to your problems by showing you how we are solving ours."

I realized that I had been relentless in my attack, but it provoked an ovation which resounded throughout those attending this meeting and to others who did not come. It was the beginning of a new attitude toward the South by the organization which, up to that time, had only been South once for a meeting. Since then, most of its meetings have been planned in southern areas.

In the midst of business consolidation concerns, I took upon myself a heavy public responsibility as president of the NAACP chapter. This burden, in 1939, occurred about the time Margaret Mitchell's *Gone With the Wind* was airing in an elaborate premier in Atlanta.

During this time, there also was an encounter with the mayor. Several of my fellow Atlantans and myself were made aware that without political input in terms of increased voter registration, the program of the NAACP would not be accomplished. Therefore, voter registration became a part of the NAACP program as it had been in the Atlanta Negro Chamber of Commerce.

In addition, there where two campaigns in which the NAACP was involved. One was the equalization of teachers' pay and the other was the removal of the prohibition against married persons being employed as teachers. These were two important victories.

I had set out to find my place in the economic mainstream of the South. I had selected the field that afforded challenge and unlimited opportunity for personal success. In the course of reaching my objectives, I discovered a great deal more about business which became more and more fascinating and to which I became dedicated. I found a great need to encourage Blacks, particularly young Black college students and graduates.

I developed a number of pet statements which represented my belief and confidence on the possibilities of young Blacks to achieve their goals in the South or any place. One I especially liked became the hallmark of most of my public utterances: The only limitations you and I need ever fear are those we are stupid enough to place upon ourselves.

While I think Blacks must struggle to earn recognition based upon ability, we must also treat our achievements with unusual care and caution so that every gain will be a permanent step forward to full acceptance, without regard to commutation of race. The Black American must try to avoid being singled out as a Black who had done something unusual. The quality and import of the contribution must defy racial identification.

For instance, as I was becoming well known in insurance circles one day I received a call from an official of a national organization asking if I would write a brief story of how I started in the insurance business and allow it to be published in the top official publication of the industry. I told him it was not much of a story, but I could sum it up in a few words:

"I had the will and desire to work hard, the determination and patience that are required to accomplish anything, and I had the cooperation and understanding that follow high purposes."

"However," I said, "I would like to contribute an article to the magazine, if you think it would be accepted." He told me to write it and send it to the publisher. I did. My article was on one of the most technical and controversial clauses in the insurance contract affecting commercial risk. It was widely read and I received many letters on it, and extra prints were requested of the publisher.

I was not identified as a Negro though many already knew it. It was the feature article of the issue in which it appeared. I was invited to send other articles at any time I wished. I had nothing else of that nature that I felt compelled to write about, therefore, I did not contribute another article.

Someone told me later that no Black had previously contributed an article to the publication. Any good insurance man could have done the same. It should be no single honor that I should know the field to which I was dedicating my life. If I could not have written my views, it would have been a reflection and a disgrace on my personal qualifications.

To highlight every unusual achievement of the Black American or add unusual significance to his commendable acts was segregation and discrimination of the worst sort. We have contributed in no small measure to our own segregation. We treated the normally expected as the unusual and over-emphasized our less commendable activities in blazing headlines. Our opponents have used both as evidence against us in our struggle for equality.

I took time out to count and share blessings. I had done very well with my earnings which I put to work and to the best use I knew. I had a son, a daughter, a devoted and patient wife, who sometimes thought my dreams fantastic, but who had long since resigned herself to expecting even the foolish ones to become true at any moment. I had done some investing in real estate at the right time in the market and cashed in on some of the profits resulting in increased value during the period just prior to the "Pearl Harbor" disaster.

I was approaching the beginning of my tenth year out of school and in business, and marriage. All my anniversaries were thirty days apart. My wife and I had been planning a new home and toward that end I had already purchased a desirable piece of land in a rapidly developing semi-suburban community. I was not quite ready to plunge into a major construction project, but I have always moved with faith and the approval of my "Upstairs Boss" whom I reverently regarded as "My Silent Partner."

God had never failed me and had always measured my shoulder before placing a cross on it. Miracles were no less possible then than they were two thousand years earlier. Our faith in His power may have weakened, but He held the world in His hand and could suspend the order of the universe at will. Everything that happened from my escaping death at the age of eleven had strengthened my faith. Once I was satisfied my direction was right, I never hesitated to move with assurance and confidence.

Meanwhile, with the United States fully committed to war after the bombing of Pearl Harbor, and with the European war continuing, the United States would have to fight on two fronts simultaneously. About this time, I was given a non-combatant Army classification narrowly missing an active role.

Normally, this would have been the worst time in my life to take any risk not forced upon me. I had already expanded my activities into Alabama and had, in rapid succession, captured the contract for insurance on construction of the 99th Pursuit Squadron Air Base at Tuskegee. I won this contract competing against more powerful White agents who wined and dined the prospect, which was something I could not do. I beat them because of the quality of service I was prepared to render.

Through a series of negotiations and setbacks, I established two branch offices in Alabama, and landed several coveted institutional accounts. I had achieved this using similar patterns and procedures I formally applied, but with less opposition. I had convinced the companies I represented that I was a safe bet and they followed me in each office expecting me to duplicate what I had done in Georgia.

I had enough companies bidding for my business that I could move without much fear of opposition. I no longer had to fight my battles alone. In fact, I often learned of a battle to stop me only after my companies had completely settled the matter for me.

In the midst of my success in the 1940s, I realized all the ills of the South affecting race relations could not be truthfully laid at the door of White Southerners. There was, however, no question as to the abundance of White responsibility for the viciousness with which Whites clung to needless prejudices. Their conscience was sufficiently loaded without the added burden of the problems which we possess a unique genius for creating. We, too, had to respect their flagrant hypocrisy combined with the sincerity with which they had promoted and defended their baseless fears and groundless prejudices - the paradoxes that confused and confounded their own conscience. They believed they were following their only path and their belief was an obsession and a compulsion from which they saw no escape.

After measuring the risks, I decided I would celebrate my tenth anniversary in a new home. I calculated the risk, and I set a timetable and a program. I looked at the best houses we could afford. I wanted our home to be symbolic of my thinking or I could never live with it. It had to reflect the personality of its occupants. It had to be more than a place in which to abide. It had to be an abiding place, a home, a sanctuary, and an inspiration to my family and to me. It had to crown ten years of faith and confidence. In other words, it had to be a living testimonial to my belief in what was possible in the segregated South.

My architect and I destroyed three sets of plans before we arrived at what we were all happy with. What we were happy with was our only concern because this was a personal matter. There was no attempt or desire to imitate or to outclass anybody. We just wanted a home in which we planned to rear our family, which stood for the projection of our own personalities and thinking.

It was nine months in construction and, in April of 1941, we moved in with everything complete in every detail, furnished, and beautifully landscaped. In July, our second daughter and third child was born.

Founding of Southeast Fidelity

One who has to depend upon an unfriendly or antagonistic source of supply for his basic tools is in an untenable position.

T.M. Alexander, Sr.

During the course of World War II, I made contributions where I was capable, such as helping to sell bonds and supporting those loved ones left behind in community-sponsored activities. I also continued to speak. One speech, *Mobilizing Youth for Peace*, I gave at First Congregational Church on April 30, 1944. I said:

"Master of Ceremonies, Ladies and Gentlemen, I confess I was deeply flattered when the responsibility which this occasion imposes was more or less thrust upon me. But as I think back over the years and remember John Pittman, that dynamic personification of youth, from whose active brain these College Nights became a vibrant reality and those illustrious speakers who from time to time graced this occasion, my ego is super-imposed upon by a sense of total inadequacy. But we must bear in mind that man power shortages is one of the tragedies of this war.

"Mobilizing youth for peace, forecast problems and difficulties far more acute than the Herculean task of mobilizing youth for war. One writer had defined peace as that period of time in which human beings toil diligently to pay for the preceding war and the succeeding one. As we look back over the pages of history, that seems to be a fairly accurate definition."

Not long after speaking at the First Congregational Church, my mother came to town. The effort I put fourth that July in making her stay a success was well rewarded. I had decked my terrace with so many flowers that many neighbors may have thought that I moved out and a florist had relocated to my address.

My house was becoming quite an attraction as more people found out that I had designed it to be a way station for those coming to Atlanta, and indeed, many people did drop by. My home was featured in several publications. One magazine, *Color* out of Charleston, West Virginia, featured it in its August 1946 issue. At this time, the article picked out a characteristic I tried to follow. I certainly gave it as advice, so why shouldn't I follow my own advice I so often gave out for free? It was stated I had a spirit of adventure and that "practically every step in Mr. Alexander's business is accurately and skillfully planned."

I was moving ahead. I had branches of my insurance business scattered in Georgia and Alabama. My friend, William Calloway, and I had been in our realty business for about one year. I was also planning to enter the construction business. I was continuing to attract so much attention that I was invited to the *Second Conference on the Negro in Business*, sponsored by the U.S. Department of Commerce, October 17, 18, and 19 in 1946.

It also was good the following year when my mother and father celebrated their 50th anniversary together in Montgomery. An article at that time called my father a "pioneer" citizen. He had been in business for 45 years. Now, retired to his home on Wetumpka Road, a Dutch colonial structure, he was overjoyed to have his family members at home to take part in the celebration. These included Alston Alexander who was in the hardwood floor business in Atlanta; my sister, Mrs. I.P. Connaly, her husband was an interior decorator; and my brother Julius, head of Security Construction Company that we had in partnership; and me.

It felt good to show my success to my father who had developed confidence in me over the years because I had successfully converted my college education into the kind of success he respected. It was always my father's practice to exhibit that trust in me by sending me to sell property for him. He gradually parcelled the land he bought on Wetumpka and I sold pieces to businesses wanting to locate there now that the city was approaching our suburban home. I once negotiated a sale for land that became a gas station and a cleaning plant. Papa would take his profit and say, "Hattie and I don't need all this money and I want to see you enjoy it while I'm alive." He would give each one of us the same amount after every sale. It must be said that I probably tried all my life to live up to my father and mother's standards.

As a revitalized post World War began in earnest, I hoped to become part of a new beginning. Knowing the needs of Blacks in the field of insurance, I was determined to launch a multi-line insurance company. Thus, my vision to launch Southeast Fidelity was born.

Like the Master said, "Sabbath was made for man and not man for Sabbath," and likewise for laws, regulations, and traditions. This was particularly true in Georgia, and especially when it was a question of following the letter of the law, or bending it in favor of progress or maybe giving it a more liberal interpretation. Sometimes the laws were drawn so that they could be interpreted to fit the occasion or with loopholes that formed escape hatches. In other words, certain specific situations could not be handled with in the law or regulations, and what was traditional, customary, or expedient was the basis for decisions. There was enough flexibility so that the final outcome could be rewarding or punishing to the recipient.

White Southerners had a tendency for paternal relationships with Blacks. It was not in a condescending way. Rather, it was their way of paying a past-due debt, satisfying their own conscience or a desire just to be helpful in a worthwhile cause.

I learned that you have to know the system and work with it, maintaining your own integrity and respect as well as that of those with whom you are dealing. There is always a mutual advantage and joint satisfaction in the accomplishment.

In 1950, I saw the need for a Black fire insurance company and convened a group of businesses and professional Blacks including Treasurer L.D. Milton, C.R. Yates, Warren Cochran, Richard Hackney, John W. Dobbs, and A.T. Walden to discuss creating such a business. We raised $200,000, which was the minimum amount required to charter a fire insurance company under the laws of Georgia. $100,000 was assigned to surplus and the other $100,000 was required for capital.

The capital had to be invested in securities prescribed by the Regulatory Department of the State, under the direction of the Insurance Commissioner and Comptroller, whose offices were in the State Capitol Building. The securities had to be deposited with the Treasurer of the State of Georgia where it could be used if the company got into financial difficulty.

This $200,000 in capital and surplus only permitted the company to operate in the State of Georgia, but not to expand into other states. Southeastern Fidelity, the name settled upon for our company, would be the first Black-owned fire insurance company ever chartered in Georgia. This was another first and a sense of pride for me.

As a matter of fact, no other state had chartered a Black fire insurance company since the North Carolina Mutual Insurance Company in North Carolina which was subsequently sold to Equitable of Florida. But our company, to be sure of sufficient business volume, needed to go into Alabama at the same time, where there were several Black-owned agencies already operating. Normally this would require an additional deposit which our group of investors did not have.

When I explained to the Commissioner, Zachary Cravey, how important it was for us to be able to go into Alabama, he reminded me of the law regarding a new company and the minimum capital and surplus we had. I told him I did not think I could proceed with the company unless I could operate in Alabama.

Agencies in Alabama from whom we had received pledges were controlled by some of our associates and stockholders. They were an essential part of our strategy for success. The Georgia Insurance Commissioner said he would make a call to the Insurance Commissioner of Alabama and see if he would agree to allow us in the state without putting up any additional money in reserve.

The call was made in my presence and he identified himself to his counterpart. From the conversation, I gathered they were good friends and members of the Organization of Insurance Commissioners.

"Yes," the Georgia Commissioner said, "I know what the law and practice is, but these folks are our best Black citizens. They have a bank, a savings and loan association, and a fine life insurance company. I trust them and they will not let me down. Okay, thanks. Anytime, I can do you a favor, all you need to do is ask. I will send you a letter stating that we will secure the State of Alabama with our deposit in case anything goes wrong. This will protect you. See you at our next annual meeting."

We were over the first hump. I thanked the Commissioner and told him he could depend on us not letting him down and we would make the state of Georgia proud of our company.

I left him to deliver my package of bonds to the State Treasurer who was at the opposite end of the building. When I presented them, he fingered through the stock, smiled and said, "I see you fellows bought all good 'ole' Georgia municipal bonds. That's nice, investing in securities of your own state." He then turned them over to examine the back of the certificates. They had no assignment and were not properly executed to be used as reserve.

He frowned and said, "You'll have to send these bonds back to have them properly issued and endorsed. This is December and you will not be able to start operating as planned in January. There are a number of counties represented here and many of their officials are already talking Christmas vacations. I would say it could be 60 to 90 days before you have them all back."

As I started to leave, I decided I would go back to the Insurance Commissioner and ask his help again. I asked him if he would go with me around to the Treasurer's office and let him explain what was wrong with the bonds. I knew what had to be done, but I was confident that somehow the two of them, being political friends, could come up with a solution.

He said, "I'll be glad when you get this company started. I've already altered one requirement for you." I thanked him again and told him I hated to bother him again, and he would not regret it.

He approached the Treasurer and they exchanged short first-name greetings, indicative of their close friendship. The Commissioner asked what was wrong with the bonds. The Treasurer said, "Nothing, good ole Georgia municipals. All they have to do is send them back to be properly executed. You know these county bonds don't operate too fast, and especially at Christmas time."

The Commissioner replied, "Yes, I know, but we want to help these good citizens out, so what can we do?"

With that, the Treasurer asked who purchased the bonds. I told him the Treasurer of the company was L.D. Milton, President of our Citizens Trust. He asked for his telephone number. We stood there while he called him. He commended him on the quality of the securities but told him buying bonds to put up for reserve was different than buying bonds for bank investments. He then asked if his bank closed and was reopened after the bank holiday during Roosevelt's administration.

Milton answered, "Yes, it was closed by order of the Banking Department even though it was solid and was paying all depositors upon request." It was one of the first to reopen because of its soundness and became a direct member of the Federal Reserve Banks. Formally, its clearings were through the Fulton National Bank, whose president was Ryburn Clay, brother of General Lucius Clay of the U.S. Army.

After this explanation, the Treasurer said, "As a member of the Federal Reserve Bank, you qualify as a depository for the State of Georgia. I will designate you today with a letter. In the meantime, after they are properly executed, I want you to hold some securities for an insurance company, until I ask for them. Send me a receipt for same. Glad to know your bank is a member of the Federal Reserve. Maybe we can make you one of our regular depositories for State funds.

This was the beginning of a lasting relationship. No one was let down and no one lost. We kept our promise to our friends and they to us. This type of relationship and trust is the genius of Atlanta and its continued progress.

With the establishment of Southeast Fidelity in 1950, I was now the head of an insurance company as well as representing other insurance companies in my agency, Alexander and Company.

Not too long after establishing Southeast Fidelity, Fred Mackey of Gary, Indiana, came into the picture. I had met Mackey some years before when he dropped by my house one day while he was down in

Atlanta to see his sister graduate. Because I treated him hospitably, he never forgot it. After we had established Southeast Fidelity, he called me one day to express his appreciation for my kindness. He also said in the course of this conversation that he had heard about our insurance company and wanted it to insure a building he owned.

The transaction was handled over the phone. The details were to be worked out in a side trip I would make on my way to a National YMCA Board meeting in Chicago. Mackey was head of Gibraltar Insurance Company and we met in the Director's Room. Mackey told me to wait there. When he returned, he had a shopping bag filled with $100,000 in cash. He said, bluntly, "Put that in your insurance company."

I told him I didn't have an escrow account, and the preemptive rights of my stockholders had not expired. I could not sell any stock to an outsider until they would give me authority to go ahead to sell to outside people. "Furthermore, I added, "I don't have anywhere to put that money."

He replied, "Well, put it in your own account."

To this, I said, just as quickly, "I would not walk out the door with that kind of cash." He then had a solution for this.

He said, "Well, I'm the biggest depositor in the bank across the street." He sent me over there with one of his men. The cash was short $20, therefore, we came back. He handed me $20 without looking. Then he said, "Now, take it back over there and get that check."

After getting the check, I came back to his office. He pulled out $15,000 extra and told me to put this in our savings and loan association. This was a lot of money to carry around, and naturally, I was very nervous. I went back to my hotel room and "slept" on the money all night. When I got back to Atlanta, I quickly deposited it into the bank.

At the time, I did not know where Mackey's money came from and, frankly, did not have any interest in knowing, although I presumed it was from Gibraltar Insurance Company, the name under which he told me to register the cash in the two accounts.

Some time later, Mackey was killed by an unknown assailant in the rear of his office in Gary, Indiana. I had been in the process of helping Mackey to recoup some business losses and settle some trouble with the IRS. Though Mackey had always been somewhat of a mystery to many people, he was a respected and dedicated citizen and family man.

Experiences,
Sharing and Shared

Not to achieve one's goal is not so bad as not having a goal
to achieve. If you aim and miss, you can take another shot.
Don't go through life aimlessly with no goals to strive for.
                                            T. M. Alexander, Sr.

Naturally, with the successful establishment of Southeast Fidelity, I attracted more and more attention and was asked to speak all over the country. I still considered speaking to the youth my special calling. Morehouse was a place I was preparing my son to enter. He was away at Palmer Memorial Institute in Sedalia, North Carolina, which was led by Charlotte Hawkins Brown. Ms. Brown, a woman of southern roots, took what she learned up north, came back south to North Carolina and established a successful private academy. I gave one particular speech of mine, before Morehouse men in this manner:

"I have never stood here without a keen sense of responsibility and today, more than ever before, the weight of that responsibility takes on added significance. I realize that I am speaking for the first time to the sons of some of my classmates and closest friends. I met some of you many years

ago in 1931 when you were the unborn dreams of a great
Morehouse father, who said with assurance, as only Morehouse men can, that you would be here in '50, '51, and '52.
I am happy, but not surprised to see we were right on! I want
you to know that coming through on-time is one of the many
geniuses of a good Morehouse man.

"We learned early at Morehouse that at the outset of a
person's career, a solemn purpose should be formed to make
the most and best of the powers given to that individual. This
purpose must carry with it the assent of reason, the approval
of conscience, and the sober judgement of intellect."

I continued to speak throughout the mid-fifties and people
continued to draw upon the business experience a group of us gained
from several efforts we initiated and promoted. Also, by 1957, major
changes were about to take place in my own life as I ran for political
office. In addition, Martin Luther King, Jr., was about to lead a
revolution in my hometown that would affect the entire world.

Recognition for endeavors in the field of business came in the form
of inclusion in Lucille Arcola Chambers, *America's Tenth Man: A
Pictorial Review of One-Tenth of a Nation Presenting the Negro
Contribution to American Life Today*. Included was a photograph of
Alexander and Company in 1931. In there also, was a pretty fair
representation of Atlanta's Black businesses. Calloway Realty was
there, Mutual Federal Savings and Loan, Citizens Trust Co., Yates-
Milton Drug Co., and The Hopkins Book Concern was mentioned,
which a group of us, Q.V. Williams, Charles Protho, and me, later
reorganized as Associated Enterprises.

Others mentioned included W.H. Aiken, who was a large
contractor. He was particularly active in the Fairview Terrace
subdivision. He also built Walahaje, the most expensive Black-owned

hotel complex. Aiken's father-in-law was H.A. Rucker, Collector of Internal Revenue for Atlanta from 1897 to 1910.

The eyes and ears of the community, the *Atlanta Daily World*, run by the Scott family and radio station WERD, one of Blayton's many interest were also given some publicity in Mrs. Chambers' book.

One speech I gave in the late 1950s was *Business and Our Tomorrow*. It was Detroit, on June 16, 1958 before the Booker T. Washington Trade Association. I stated:

"I want to share with you some points of view which I think you and I must inevitably come to grips with and adopt as accepted policy and procedure if we are to be a part of the mainstream of the American economy. I want to preface my remarks with a description of the three classes of people we have to encounter in any attempt to move from mediocrity or the status-quo to new plateaus of economic, political, or social responsibility.

"Throughout history, change has been accompanied by disturbance and unrest. Men and nations either rise to greater heights of valor and character or sink to unprecedented depths of brutality and cowardice. In such a time, there is a sharp shifting of the goat and the sheep, no individual, no race, and no nation can escape the process. In such a time, there also emerges three groups with at least three points of views relative to the course to be followed. They emerged in the wilderness with Moses and they are no less imminent today.

"First, there are those who resent change and the adjustments and the discipline which new concepts impose. They cling blindly to the past and, like the children of Israel, would rather go back to the fleshpots of Pharaoh and enslave their children's children than sacrifice and earn the freedom abundance of a Promised Land.

"The second group aren't quite willing to return to the enslavement of yesteryears, but neither are they adventurous enough to move forward to the freedom of tomorrow. They are the let-well-enough-do-crowd or let's just be satisfied with what we've got and where we are. They're willing to stand by and let whosoever will go forward, clear the way, solve the problems, make the rough places smooth and the crooked straight. With this assurance, once it's safe and the objective has been secured, they will organize a great phalanxes and move in one great mass and help enjoy the spoils of victory.

"The last group, I call the Creative Minority, and since the beginning of time, they have always been in the minority. These are the ones who have accomplished everything. They have accomplished the welfare of the world, and passed onto unborn generations a legacy of respectability, hope, and courage, that has lifted them from the malarious damps of the lowlands, out of inertia and inarticulate concern, into the sunlight of boundless horizons.

"It is this Creative Minority to which you and I must belong. I shall try to give you some idea of the philosophy of this group and the course it must chart for itself on the economic front as it struggles to raise itself to a higher plateau in American life."

Naturally, I was more than eager to speak before the Dallas Negro Chamber of Commerce Banquet on February 27, 1959, where my uncle, R.T. Hamilton, had been a presence. On this occasion, I said:

"I should like to seriously share with you an economic philosophy borne out of my strong belief in the free enterprise system, which avoids both compromise for the sake of expediency and wishful thinking to avoid the unpleasant. I want to raise two questions in my subject.

* Economic Respectability or Economic Mediocrity?
* Economic Determination or Economic Determinism?

"One rather facetious, but valid definition of Economic Darwinism is: When your outgo exceeds your income, and your upkeep is your downfall, you are like the man who jumped out of a 20-story building and changed his mind as he passed the 10 floor. His doom was sealed when he jumped. Present company excepted, of course.

"We proceed in Atlanta from three major premises, and whatever else I say this evening I submit these three points to your thinking because we must fasten our seat belts for the turbulent weather ahead, and you will have to set your goal by stars you cannot see, and dig for water springs with the divining rod that you may reach. Hence, I am giving you the summary before I give the speech.

"Number one, the most dangerous and untenable position in which you and I or any race or ethnic group or nation can find itself is to have to depend upon an antagonist or unfriendly source of supply for any basic need.

"Number two, you and I will attain neither economic respectability, nor social or political respectability, as long as we come to the banquet table with nothing but the appetite. As the old deacon says in his prayer in *God's Trombones*, "Lord, we come to thy ever flowing and abundant fountain bringing our empty pitchers." We must cease going to the fountain, economically or otherwise, with empty pitchers. It is stupid and inconsistent to demand with one hand and beg with the other.

"Number three, there is no economic therapy that can immunize you and me from the sanctum and the sovereignty of the marketplace. We stand on the threshold of the greatest era in the history of mankind, and at no point in our lives have the opportunities been more abundant, the risk so great, and never before have you and I been more challenged. A whole new world of human relationships and economics is struggling with agonizing birth pains to be born.

"Our miraculous stride in science and technology baffles our most fantastic dreams. Our economic progress and material wealth seem an inexhaustible storehouse constantly replenished by our canny skill and genius. Never before have we been better fed, better clothed, better educated, and better housed; and never before have we been as confounded, confused, and complex as we are today.

"Many of our problems are self-inflicted, and the worst failure in the world is failure in the presence of great opportunities. I say to you with firmness of conviction, the only limitations that you and I need to ever fear are those we are stupid enough to place upon ourselves.

"I grant you, we have been in a game where the referee was often partial and unfair; where the glory, the honor, and reward frequently went to those who have lied, cheated, and bribed. We have seen the wicked, as unfit, exalted to places of power and trust. We have seen unselfishness, decay, and service rewarded by bitterness and hate lead to heartbreak by the cold hand of ingratitude. We have seen our long-cherished dreams for justice, respect, and equality fade into the merciless sunlight of reality.

"Yet, through a thousand midnights of abuse, economic pressure, political ostracism, and social chaos, we have somehow managed to keep before your vagrant step the kindly light of hope amid the tempest and turbulence of the changing years. No racial or ethnic group in history has risen to such a height from as great a depth, in as short a time, with so much against it as has the American Negro. We can appreciate the height to which we have come when we remember the depths from which we came. We must not become complacent or relaxed because we have a greater distance to go. As Alice in Wonderland said, "We must run faster than all the rest, just to keep up!"

"So, it is groups like yours, the Chamber of Commerce, and similar committee groups and organizations which keep us alert so that we will not become overwhelmed by a few successes, and therefore, consider them as citadels of immunity where we may remain secure. We, again, reach another level of responsibility in which we are obligated to make good.

"There is no economic therapy or statement of high resolve that can immunize you or me from the sanctum and sovereignty of the marketplace. I don't care what your assets are in the material wealth and mental resource aspects. Unless these can be correlated to the service of the community and to the public, it would be better if you didn't have them. We have got to measure up to a single standard of efficiency and service in the free enterprise system or we will forever remain on the outer fringes of the economic picture. There is no 'big me' and 'little you'. We must pool all of our resources, materials, and mental abilities to gain the respect that will enable us to walk the streets with the dignity of American citizens.

"There is some little Negro boy, who, given the opportunity of education and development in the free enterprise system, could shoot a rocket around the moon without getting up a sweat. God is a great decreer of equality and He is impartial with His distribution of talents."

T.M. standing in new home built in 1941.

Standing in front of father's home in 1940.

Mother Hattie, grandmother Clara, and T.M. Sr., holding T.M. Jr.

Parents, James Henry and Hattie Mable Alexander during 50th Anniversary celebration.

Children - Alvia, Dorothy, and T.M. Jr.

Two story office building built by T.M. Sr., in 1946 which housed his insurance agency and the real estate brokerage business. This building was sold when desegregation allowed T.M. to move into a business district.

T.M. and L.D. Milton, long time friend, business associate, and teacher. Milton was President of Citizens Trust Bank.

(Above) T.M., accompanied by his wife, Dr. Lenora Cole-Alexander, being sworn in for a six year appointment in 1983 to the African Development Foundation. (Below) Vacation time!

Black
Housing in Atlanta

A wise man may be a cultured man or a fool. Wisdom is to know a thing, but culture is to dignify it.

T.M. Alexander, Sr.

In many southern cities, the impact of industrialization, farm mechanization, and labor unionization brought along with its advantages, many inescapable problems. None had been more acute than the housing problem of minorities, generally aggravated by the traditional pattern of segregation and discrimination.

Few southern cities had faced this problem with greater courage and a higher degree of statesmanship than Atlanta. This progress did not evolve by accident, nor can any single set of circumstances or incidents be pinpointed as the spark that set off this eager, honest search for a new solution to an old problem. As in most instances, the simplicity and utter obviousness of the answer was frightening. We were sometimes inclined to even doubt its existence, when we realized how close we had always been to it, being too blind or too stubborn to see.

Housing in the South for the Black minority had followed a

consistent pattern with very little deviation. A look at maps prepared by the Metropolitan Planning Commission revealed a "crazy quilt" pattern, indicative of the lack of planning and over a half a century of gross neglect in good community development. The purpose of these maps and other studies made by our city in cooperation with other governmental and private agencies was an indication of our determination to act on the facts we had discovered.

Blacks and Whites had always lived as neighbors in the South. Before Emancipation, they lived on the same lot, same farm, and frequently in the same house. This was considered not only desirable, but was demanded for convenience and economic reasons. So accustomed was the South to this pattern, and without friction, that it was given up with great reluctance. In some rural sections throughout the South, the pattern prevailed, and not infrequently in urban areas where the status-quo could be maintained.

During the Reconstruction Period, little "pockets" of Black communities were dotted like piles of rubbish in every White community in all sections of the city. It was planned that way. The Black Americans, being basically engaged in services and unskilled labor, were encouraged and assisted in developing a community in close proximity to their places of employment or within calling distance of the "big house." Sometimes Blacks were given a plot of ground, a small farm or a small house to assure this accustomed convenience.

The Black Americans have always been a potent factor in the economy of the South and could no more escape the benefits from it than they could escape its evils. All the members of a democratic society enjoyed the economic fortunes and suffered the misfortunes of that society, no matter how segregated or circumscribed they may be. Maybe not in equitable proportions, but, if the South made great strides economically, the Blacks always advanced because whether we chose to or not, we were tied together by a common destiny. In any community where the White population was derelict and backward, so was the Black population. Any community where the White population was prosperous, so was the Black population.

Because of marked similarity, we always followed a parallel line which sometimes crossed and often threatened to meet. No one person could be given the credit for our beautiful homes and numerous subdivisions. In fact, these homes were the result of many Blacks and Whites working together rather than against each other. Certainly the Empire Real Estate Board (EREB), of which I was president from 1945 to 1953 could not take full credit, even though the organization had played a major role.

In 1939, a group of Black real estate brokers of Atlanta were denied membership in the Atlanta Realtors Board, and as a result, formed their own organization, the Empire Real Estate Board. They were W.H. Aiken, John S. Allen, O.T. Bell, Wendall Cunningham, Roger Henderson, N.D. Jones, and J.R. Wilson, Jr. They elected W.H. Aiken as their first president.

By 1944, most of the organizers had retired from business and the board, to an extent, had ceased to function. That year, Bob Wilson, Jr., one of the remaining active EREB founders, convened a meeting of a new generation of real estate brokers in his office to reactivate the organization. At that meeting, I, a partner in the firm of Alexander-Calloway Realty Company, was elected President of the new Board.

Under my administration, the Board, after being completely restructured, began functioning regularly, on a monthly basis. The Empire Real Estate Board grew and played a key role in the field of housing, especially for minorities.

Many of Atlanta's outstanding leaders have served as President of EREB. Some of them were-

Q.V. Williamson   1954-1959

J.T. Bickers	1960-1962
W.L. Calloway	1963-1965
R.T. Robie	1966
Allen Caldwell	1967
J.A. Alston	1968
Otis Thorpe	1969
Harold A. Dawson	1970-1972
W.D. Ponder	1973
Willie Ware	1975
Willie R. Jackson, III	1977
Miller Johnson, Jr.	1979-1981
E. Pearl Presley	1982

The most significant move toward better housing for Blacks started back in the early 1920s, during the time of Hemon Perry and the Standard Life and Service Company. Whatever errors of judgement or administration that overtook this big combine of grocery stores, dry goods stores, banking, insurance, and so on, its impact for good was exceeded only by the fact that it no longer existed in its original corporate form. The spirit and the intent had never been liquidated nor had it bankrupted the minds of Atlanta's Blacks to reconstruct from their ashes a sounder foundation upon which to build.

Many who saw this empire fade away were younger men in minor positions who had profited by the mistakes they saw made. These young men went on to build enterprises and institutions of unquestioned soundness and character. These institutions, and the men who guided them were not "after-thought" businessmen. They were well-trained and disciplined for their jobs and their responsibilities to the community. They served as an inspiration, as well as an economic force. They were the practical dreamers whose tools and money, balance sheets and profit-and-loss statements, and character and integrity were good for the community.

Men such as A.F. Herndon, were the types eager to witness the raising of the monument of Booker T. Washington in 1922 at Tuskegee. Their counterparts from throughout the South, such as C.C. Spaulding, were there also, rubbing shoulders with the White corporate might, which sustained Tuskegee and endowed it. This was highly instructive to those visiting the huge, well-built backdrop of Tuskegee Institute.

No one person controlled the economic resources of Blacks in Atlanta, as Booker T. Washington did in Tuskegee. After all, Atlanta was more diverse with many more people and opportunities. We operated in a free money market and competed on the basis of our ability to compete. There were three main economic "wheels" which provided additional economic force at the time and place needed. These wheels turned separately or together, independent, yet coordinated as the situation demanded, but they never pulled in opposite directions.

The Atlanta Life Insurance Company represented one, Citizen Trust Company represented another, and Mutual Federal Savings and Loan represented a third. Together, in the 1940s, they represented more than $100 million of economic "responsibility" for Atlanta's Blacks. Because of this unique situation, money for legitimate purposes was available indiscriminately, and free competition existed for good customers across racial lines. This was the basis of housing and other economic progress found in Atlanta.

Atlanta Blacks, like Blacks in other cities in the South, followed patterns of expanding into housing vacated by Whites during an early period of growth. There were no shortages of land, but land had to be politically cleared for Black expansion, or housing tensions would arise causing bad race relations. Therefore, enlightened leadership of both races worked to bring about the orderly and peaceful expansion of housing for all citizens.

This had not come about without some tension and opposition, however, the majority opinion had prevailed in most instances. The City Government had been cooperative and friendly in making city services available in new development areas. Neighborhood committees and an Overall Citizens Committee of both races had worked to peacefully settle expansion problems where tensions arose. This type of cooperation had contributed toward clearing the way for Black housing expansion.

One of the most important factors, however, had been the foresight, leadership, and the financial resources which individual Blacks themselves had made available. The sources of our basic needs had not been antagonistic to our program of progress toward a higher plateau of economic respectability. Housing had been but one of the dramatic facets in which this fact had been expressed. Although the process we were using was not unique, it was being applied to a successful end. I knew of other situations, say, for instance, in Durham and Houston where a similar kind of dynamism and responsibility produced good housing and an independent, vibrant Black business community. You could find help and assistance if you were willing first to help yourself and wisely use your own resources before asking to risk the resources of other fellows.

Following World War II, the major problems facing the country was inadequacy of housing in urban areas, for everyone. The federal government, in rapid sequence, set up a number of housing agencies, such as The Federal Housing Administration, Public Housing Administration, and Veterans Housing Administration. A variety of commissions and commissioners were established or appointed to administer the job of providing emergency housing for returning veterans as well as a civilian population too busy with war production to house itself.

Housing was a national problem. Slums had increased with all its attending evils, such as delinquency, crime, and increased death rates. This was not a pretty sight with which to greet homesick, war-worn veterans.

In Atlanta, Wilson Wyatt was given the task in 1947 of stimulating action to relieve the emergency housing situation. Atlanta got off at the "shot of the gun." The Atlanta Chamber of Commerce at the time was under the leadership of Attorney Elbert P. Tuttle, eventually Federal Judge Tuttle. The Chamber had a housing committee which was already at work on Atlanta's housing problem. The mayor immediately designated this existing committee as the Emergency Housing Committee which was asked to assume a larger and overall responsibility. A small group of Blacks were invited to a meeting at the Chamber of Commerce office.

Each group present tried to project its immediate and future housing needs. At this meeting, it was pointed out that one-third of the Black population occupied approximately 10 percent of the available land. In addition, the Black population was growing so rapidly that the "small pocket communities" it occupied were bursting at the seams. Not only did the Blacks need immediate housing relief - they needed land for future expansion and community development. Someone said that the pattern of growth the Black community had followed for years was conceded not to be in the best interest of race relationships. A few houses were being constructed by individual Blacks, but the number was negligible.

For the most part, the great masses were poorly and inadequately housed with no immediate relief apparent. Considerably more was being done to relieve the housing problem among Whites. As better housing became available for the non-Black population, those who could afford it moved, leaving their second-hand housing either for other less fortunate Whites or to Black occupancy. Because the Black demand for housing was greater than the second-hand supply, the opportunity to get a few extra dollars from the Black market set off a spark of economic exploitation that almost got out of control.

To say the least, many of the Black communities in Atlanta were formerly occupied by Whites. The housing profile of our city changed considerably in the last half century. As strange as it sounds, Whites moving out and Blacks moving in, was the only available solution. Blacks had neither new housing nor sufficient available land on which to build. Those who owned the land would not sell for Black housing. Every Black community was "bottled in" on all sides. There were two ways out - which were to expand into the White community or "leap-frog" into the suburban areas, where again, you met another White community. Something had to give and nothing seemed inclined to.

This was the beginning of housing tensions and a misconception that harassed racial goodwill. There were malicious damages of all sorts, such as fires, cross-burnings, "night shirt" parades, bombs, and what-have-you. This embarrassed and tormented the life out of Blacks who wanted but one thing - decent housing in which to rear their children into respectable, useful citizens. Blacks were forgotten for decades by neglectful city fathers who seemed completely oblivious to the needs, the aspirations, and the future well-being of one-third of the city's population.

"When you sow the wind, you often reap the whirlwind," and the ghost of our neglect came back to haunt us.

Housing conditions began to show improvement for minorities in Atlanta under the Roosevelt Administration and the advent of public housing which replaced many of Atlanta's worst slum areas. The local city government, under the progressive and enlightened leadership of Mayor William B. Hartsfield, did more in a few years to eradicate slums and ghettos than all the other administrations combined.

In some areas, you were unable to tell exactly where the White community stopped and the Black community began. The Black community was identifiable, however, where there were no side-walks, unpaved streets, inadequate street lighting, infrequent garbage collection, and numerous other objectionable occurrences.

The Black community had been concerned but had not been able to make its concerns articulate. Petitions, requests, and appeals had gone unheeded. The few so-called "exclusive" residential sections were unprotected either by inadequate zoning laws or lack of enforcement of existing laws. Stores, factories, liquor stores, and trucking firms, popped up next door to or across from some of the best residences in the city owned by Blacks.

For example, appeal after appeal went before the zoning boards only to be denied. Blacks lost heavily in the depreciations of their property values. Many, too deeply entrenched financially to move, found themselves living in second-rate commercial areas. There was no suburban land available and Blacks lived in the thickly populated urban area. Even inside the city limits you could not always be sure of all the necessary utilities that made healthy, wholesome living.

This, in itself, put a premium on all adjacent White communities and increased the potential of racial tension. If Blacks could move into a section previously occupied by Whites, they could be sure of paved streets, transportation facilities to and from work, proper street lighting, and all the normal conveniences to which all citizens are entitled. Blacks willing to pay a premium, if the prices paid can be classified, as such served sometimes to induce a bit of greed on the part of his "neighbor."

There was a gross misconception that generally prevailed when Blacks began to move into houses made available in borderline or White communities. It wasn't at all true that Blacks were particularly concerned or interested in moving next to or in close proximity to Whites. It was simply that these communities afforded those conveniences to which they were entitled in their own communities and had been denied. Also, it did not follow that Blacks who moved from the slums or an inferior crime-infested environment would bring into a new community the characteristics of their old environment.

When the first Black public housing project was being considered in Atlanta, it was reputedly said that it would be a waste of money to build such a development; that Blacks would be cutting wood on the floors and making booze or storing coal in the bathtubs. However, once that particular project was finished, it became one of the best kept in the city and received fewer police calls.

In private housing, Black home owners had not depreciated the value of property they acquired from Whites and, in most instances, enhanced its value by improving it and planting grass and flowers where weeds were. Blacks had always had a latent love for beauty but too few opportunities to express it. Not only had Blacks been denied expression of his appreciation of beauty but more importantly, denied expression of his political opinions with even greater vigilance and severity.

Blacks, as well as their White neighbors, had been derelict about registering and voting. A major reason was the so-called "White Primary" and poll tax which disfranchised both races. After the removal of these two evils, and through constant prodding by dedicated leadership, Blacks finally began to wake up to the value of the ballot. They discovered that it wouldn't take too many votes to make their one-third population strength a balance of power. In a few significant local elections, the vote spelled the difference. This was the beginning of a turning point and a new and wholesome concept of Blacks in the City of Atlanta.

Of course, paralleling this new political interest was a quiet, persistent, and sound economic development sponsored by Blacks, initiated by Blacks, and controlled by Blacks, much earlier than the acquisition of political power a second time around. (Blacks had been very political after the Civil War.) No city in America could match the economic progress of Blacks in Atlanta. The racial good will and cooperation on the economic level were the most fantastic and fascinating stories of American enterprise and genius.

The focal points around which this remarkable advance had been soundly constructed were the insurance companies, banks, strong financial, educational, and spiritual institutions. To demand political and economic respect, one had to have political and economic respectability. These were the two keys that helped to open the door where old neighbors began to take a new look.

Immediately following that original meeting in the Chamber of Commerce's office under Elbert P. Tuttle, the news got out, and the "land-grabbers" immediately went to work. Blacks were expanding in an orderly and logical direction out Simpson Road, westward toward the river. Just ahead of this Black development and directly in its path was the creation of a new White community to the west of Hightower Road, the area generally known as Collier Heights. This, along with other vacant land owned by Whites, afforded another "road block" to Black housing expansion. When all the available land was utilized, Blacks again found themselves bottled in on all sides.

The West Lake area, because of its proximity to the new developments, was willingly relinquished to Walter Aiken, a Black developer. This area, and the development toward Mozley Park, laid Mozley Park open to a natural pincer movement. It became a wedge-shaped White community between two fully developed Black communities, both bursting at the seams. The untimely "road block" boomeranged and shifted the pressure from the west toward the south, and Mozley Park was literally pinched out of existence as a White community. This did not happen without incidents and some rather amusing and rather disgusting tactics.

Blacks were one block of Mozley Park on Hunter Road, where I lived. Hunter Road became Mozley Drive with the first house occupied by Whites. The Hunter Road sign was shifted, block by block, as Blacks approached Mozley Park, until they occupied too much of it to move it any further. The street names were used interchangeably. Blacks and Whites obviously were not supposed to live on streets bearing the same name even though they did.

A few new organizations were formed in the community under the leadership of professional agitators, the Columbians. A few crosses were burned, a few homes visited, and a few dollars were collected by the leaders to prevent the shift-over. A few real estate brokers, myself and partner Calloway included, had their licenses cancelled on trumped-up charges which could be made to stick legally, such as "misrepresentation."

But Mozley Park went as had others before it. In fact, Ralph McGill of the *Atlanta Constitution Newspaper* easily recognized Calloway and I were being made scapegoats and wrote an editorial to this effect. Anyway, it was not too long before we recovered our licenses. Nevertheless, Mozley, the school and the park with its swimming pool, when taken over by Blacks, gave them their third swimming pool in the City of Atlanta.

Some of the Whites were slow to move and some held out for extorted prices, and many got them. Some did not move and seemed content with their new found neighbors. All sorts of pressures were used to maintain this area as a White community. Financial institutions were requested not to finance the purchase of homes for Blacks in Mozley Park. The Blacks' own financial institutions broke that bottleneck by making the first loans and ended up competing with every financial institution in the city for the mortgage business.

I initially secured financing from Atlanta Life, Citizens Trust, and Mutual Savings and Loan Association. When the White institutions thought they might be left out of this business, they gladly began to lend money to Black home buyers and this economic key opened the door. This business turned out to be some of the best in the mortgage portfolios of the local lending institutions.

The mayor was erroneously accused of having promised Mozley Park to the Blacks and was threatened with political reprisals at the ballot box come next election. The truth of the matter was the community itself was split into two factions. Some wanted to sell and others did not or pretended not to want to sell. The ones in the block immediately next to the Black community objected to forming a "buffer" for their neighbors, hence they sold first. The following block took the same position as the first, and they followed in order.

A committee of White home owners went to the Black brokers at a called meeting, with the press and police present, to express their determination to sell. When the Empire Real Estate Board, with more than 100 brokers and salesmen, refused to get in the situation at the beginning, a non-member sold an entire block without difficulty. Finally, when it became definite that the community would go, the Black brokers sold out in less than a year and the following year the park and school were turned over to Blacks.

There exist some interesting stories surrounding the "Conquest" of Mozley Park. As it became certain, many Whites panicked and many became anxious to sell to get the top dollar while the getting was good and they did not want to be the last to go. One Sunday, while driving a Black client around, a White lady stood out motioning to us excitedly to, "Come look at our house!"

In another instance, one White lady, to indicate her resolve to stay, stood guard at her property saying to any and all. "Don't stop here! Don't stop here. Our house is not for sale."

I was showing one house to a lady from Decatur, and she said to the owner, "Us don't want your house. It ain't got no picture window." There had developed a taste in Atlanta for houses with big picture windows where persons would set a beautiful table or just as beautiful a lamp which, when lit at night, would be the ultimate personal statement a home owner would make to his neighbors.

It was discovered in this experience that this pattern of expansion was not only costly financially but, more importantly, it was costly in good racial relationships. The Metropolitan Planning Commission had been organized by an Act of Legislature for the purpose of studying and replanning the entire City of Atlanta and designating land uses, highways, and connectors commensurate with a city literally bursting at the seems with an ever-increasing population and growing industrial potency.

The first report of this commission entitle, *Up Ahead*, attempted to project a picture of Atlanta progressively for 50 years. Because there was little land left available for minority group housing, certain areas in different sections of Greater Atlanta were designated as "Negro Housing Expansion areas." Immediately, this suggestion was attacked vigorously by Whites on one side who owned the land referred to and objected to the aide of relinquishing it for Black housing and on the other hand by Blacks who resented the designation of segregated areas of Black homes in the face of the Supreme Court decision. The segregated areas for Black housing was based on a plan that was supposed to foresee the picture 50 years hence. The Atlanta Black community had been grossly misreported by an Urban League office, that was consulted on the report and indicated it did not think Blacks would object to it.

One particularly objectionable part of the *Up Ahead* report was serious consideration to relocate the Auburn Avenue Black business district. This was considered especially insulting and insensitive. Comparable White business interests would not have been treated so cavalierly. I spoke out on this point, authorized to do so by the Empire Real Estate Board on June 3, 1952, before the Metropolitan Planning Commission.

The progressive element among Negroes anticipated the abolition of all segregation and discrimination in housing and other areas in less than half a century. Both sides contended that they were justified in their criticism of the plan on the basis of their respective interests.

The mayor then appointed Blacks as members of an advisory committee to the Metropolitan Planning Commission which they accepted only as an emergency measure until there were vacancies whereby they could be accepted into full membership. This, at least, afforded an opportunity for Blacks to be in on the planning rather than being planned for.

The pressure for more housing was still present, and after the War, new industries moving southward, continued to attract labor from outside the area and away from the rural sections. With all available land being developed or occupied as housing for Blacks, the Mozley Park situation set off a pattern. The feeling abroad was, if you want to get out of your present community and get a good, new, modern home, capitalize on the Black market. They're short on housing and will pay the best price.

At the same time, the developers of White housing had overdone their job of providing new subdivisions for Whites through liberal VA and FHA financing, windfalls included, and the supply was in excess of demand. As people heard of the excess housing, in a somewhat cunningly manner, rumors began to spread: This section is zoned for colored. Negroes are going to move here or there. The mayor or the Planning Commission, (or anybody who could be named) has designated this area for Negroes.

It isn't certain where or how the rumor started, but a lot of Black people started looking for new homes in the available White subdivision and Black brokers were urged to get a fast sale for White houses so that the purchase of a new one could be concluded. This started another wave of tensions because there were always those who had their doubts and were unwilling to move on rumors. This again caused communities to split and neighbors to lose friendship. The Blacks represented a ready market, but they were always caught in the community crossfire.

The main spots of tension were in the West End section of Atlanta, where Blacks had moved to the north side of Westview Drive and Whites still occupied the south side. Immediately, the Whites began to offer their houses for sale to Blacks and a few were sold. The West End community went up in arms against the Administration for permitting the invasion of this rather large community. It was at this point that the mayor, along with other citizens of both races, decided to take positive action.

The mayor appointed a six-man committee, composed of three White citizens and three Black citizens from the West End area of Atlanta. This committee was to act only in an advisory capacity to work with the citizens in the community involved in an effort to agree on the peaceful and orderly development of the White and Black communities on the west side. The committee was called the Mayor's West Side Mutual Development Committee. The Director of the Metropolitan Planning Commission was named Technical Advisor. This was a new and timely approach to a problem which was increasing in intensity as Atlanta's population expanded beyond its capacity to adequately and equitably house both races.

The first meeting was "cold" and cautious. There was a definite lack of mutual understanding and sympathy on both sides. The forced handshakes were limp and without warmth. There was even a feeling of inner tension and resentment, and a wall so thick between the groups on opposite sides of the table that it was almost visible.

The purpose of the committee was explained carefully and concisely. It was the general feeling of the mayor that if we could sit together and take an objective look at our mutual problems as intelligent citizens, we might be able to work out a solution. It would have to be a matter of give-and-take with mutual respect and equitable consideration for each. This committee would attempt to work out its difficulties on a community basis, handling each problem on its merit unemotionally and without prejudice.

It was carefully pointed out that zoning for racial groups was unconstitutional and that no one could prohibit by law any person from buying a home in any section of the city and moving in it. Further, the city law was encumbered with the responsibility of protecting this right of any citizen along with other property rights which were equally enjoyed by all races. However, both races were inclined to cooperate to protect the rights of each and respect the "integrity" of existing communities, without relinquishing any of their own rights.

This "integrity" of communities carried certain implications which should be clarified at this point. It had become a sort of "basis for understanding" in the past few years and originated with the West Side Mutual Development Committee. It became a kind of yardstick to determine to what length each group could go cooperatively and, at the same time, avoid obviating any of its legal rights or setting a pattern of procedure that looked like compromising basic principles.

A community which has "integrity" as defined by that committee was a complete, homogeneous community. It was a community composed of neighbors who were accustomed to living together, and whose children go to the same schools, churches, and parks. It had its own shopping center and a variety of homes in various classes. It had potential growth, and development was already in progress. It was not a "fringe" or "pocket" community nor tied into any other community of similar character. It was like a small town within itself.

West End was that kind of community, and so was Adamsville. Yet even communities with "integrity" would have boundaries, and could not go on indefinitely. On the other hand, nor could its "integrity" be jeopardized to the point where the community stopped. This definition applied to both racial groups and in some instances, to them jointly.

With this as a new and basic concept, with some degree of accuracy, the committee could now define communities and solicit mutual cooperation in protecting them, not against just the matter of Blacks moving into basically White communities, or vice versa, but to protect them from anything that might change their basic character or disrupt the homogeneous quality that made its existence possible.

This was the only basis upon which the committee could

honorably proceed with its work. Each member of the group represented a constituency which had to agree upon any recommendation coming from the committee. Civic organizations and professional organizations had to be sold on the general idea and on specific recommendations for them to be effective. Therefore, any suggestion had to be in the mutual interest and free from any attempt at intimidation or illegal restraint.

The first and most difficult job was to bring the committee together on its true function. This was a far cry from what they had in mind when they were called together. The early meetings were consumed by attempts to clarify and correct numerous misconceptions relative to housing expansion of minorities and the legal aspects of attempted restrictions based upon race. Again and again, the committee had to be reminded that there was no compulsion on the part of Blacks to refrain from buying property owned by Whites, and that they could not buy it if it was not put on the market for sale. It was also impossible to require a White person to refrain from selling his own property to whomever he wished, even if it affected the total community in which his property existed.

It was emphasized that the initiative to protect one's community must emanate from the community itself and not from those outside who had their own special reasons for wanting a community to remain one way or the other. The committee concluded that it was unfair, unjust, and inappropriate to ask real estate brokers to refrain from selling or accepting for sale property which was placed on the market by the owner with specific instructions which were not in violation of the law and within his property rights.

It is interesting how custom and practice can become so much a part of a pattern that it is continued by many as though it is the law rather than tradition. When any group persists in enforcing customs in solving any problem, thereby disregarding the legal rights of others, the application of the law meets with resistance patterns; if followed long enough, it eventually will be accepted as law. Hence, considerable time had to be spent in differentiating one from the other.

Gradually, with patience and an honest effort on the part of every member of the committee to define and isolate every problem objectively, the coldness began to melt away. The committeemen began to look and act like statesmen, dedicated to the job of finding answers to the perplexing problems which finally were considered as mutual responsibility. Members began to know and understand each other and respect all points of views and to face them with courage and conviction.

Many who came before the committee with problems were amazed at the relationship and mutual respect which the members had for each other. Everyone was relaxed and casual and occasionally spent a little time discussing things of general interest locally or nationally, while waiting to get to some particular problem. Points of views were exchanged on politics, sports, interesting experiences, travel, or anything that might come up. The whole atmosphere was one of congeniality. We had been neighbors a long time but spent very little time or had too few opportunities to get acquainted and herein lies the basis for most of our racial problems.

Few members of the committee had ever thought of how and why housing for minorities in the South presented a problem. Few, if any, knew the population ratio and the disparity in the allocation of land available for housing. Practically none had ever given thought to the real reason for Blacks readily agreeing to purchase houses in communities formerly occupied by Whites or in borderline areas. No one dared to openly admit that for years. Black housing in the South was stagnated, and ghettos were perpetuated by the same forces which controlled the financial institutions.

It was difficult, even in Atlanta, for a Black to borrow more than $5,000 on any house, and it was conceded that with rare exceptions, no Black was worth more than $5,000. This situation prevailed in many southern cities where there were no Black owned financial institutions to take the initiative in exploding the myth that Blacks were not a good mortgage risk. In some smaller southern cities, even with Federal aid, you could not get decent housing for minorities.

The ghettos were owned by those who had a vested interest in the banks to whom they would have to appeal for loans. The supply of Black housing was controlled and limited to insure the income of the landlord. Any outside attempts to correct this evil were met with strong opposition.

The municipalities had been derelict in their responsibility to the total community by permitting this practice to persist. It had pampered and narrowed its tax base, permitting usable land to be vacant and collected menial taxes on slums which had a potential yield that could lift the entire economic level of the community.

Hence, everybody suffered in the long run. Blacks suffered for lack of housing, high death rates, and crime. The majority of the Whites were exploited by paying the bigger end of the tax bill of the few. And the total community was deprived by lack of development and progress which an adequate tax base would have made possible.

Atlanta came to realize this, and no city in the South was growing as rapidly and had potential so incalculable as it moved progressively to provide for all its citizens indiscriminately. The "Mayor's Committee," as it was sometimes called, contributed quietly but effectively toward making Atlanta the model city of the South and set a new pattern for approaching our common problems.

The committee members frequently contacted each other between sessions on matters of mutual interest and concern. For example, a White committee member would call one of the Black members and inquire what his position was relative to a proposed liquor store in or near a Black community or he might suggest calling a meeting to discuss some proposed transition or change in a community which might be of concern to both groups. Suggested action prior to a problem was often made possible by this free exchange of ideas.

At one meeting called for the purpose of considering a subdivision development promoted by Whites for Black occupancy, the idea was discouraged by the entire committee because it was not in keeping with the character of the community and would present future problems. The promoters took the position the committee was in violation of the constitutional rights of the Blacks to try to prevent this project. The quarrel was between the White promoters and the White members of the committee on the rights of Blacks to live any place.

Obviously, it was a matter of economics in this case, which very often determined the presence or absence of more honesty. They were advised that the Black members of the committee were fully conscious of their rights and had no intention of relinquishing them. This committee was a citizens' committee and simply tried to advise steps which would ensure the peaceful, orderly, and equitable expansion of all communities on the West Side.

This proposed expansion could neither be recommended by the committee nor could the committee prevent the developers from exercising their property rights to proceed. When all the facts were made known, the project was withdrawn and the promoters agreed that the committee was right.

On another occasion, a White civic club objected to a Black development in a certain area and it came before the committee for advice. The committee convinced them they were in error and their objections to it were contrary to the principles of fair play. They agreed and withdrew their objections.

A commercial development was seeking a permit to enter a section being developed by Blacks. The White and Black citizens of the community joined forces to prevent it due to it being against the interest of the Black property owners.

In one community that was divided on whether it would sell to Blacks or not, the committee suggested that they send out a questionnaire and find out what the majority opinion was. When the reports were in, it was overwhelmingly in favor of selling to Blacks. The transition from White to Black was made over a period of a few months without friction and with complete cooperation of the entire community.

With the committee acting in an advisory capacity, violence was limited, resulting in only minor tensions that were usually reconciled through negotiations and discussions on a community level. Many situations were satisfactorily handled that might have proved embarrassing to the community and done irreparable damage to racial relations as had occurred in many southern cities.

The Run for Public Office

There are two types of people in the community, the thermometer type and the thermostat type. One reflects what the social climate is; the other adjusts it to what it should be.
T.M. Alexander, Sr.

Decades had passed since the Cotton States Exposition, held in 1895, when the last two Blacks served on the Aldermanic Board of Atlanta. Now, the question to be asked was, "Is the city of Atlanta in 1957, ready to have a Black reform city government?"

Between that long forced hiatus from elected representation, Blacks had gained some control in the Republican Party in Georgia, and in fact, in many southern cities and states. Thus, when Republicans won nationally, Blacks had control of Federal patronage. H.A. Rucker, father-in-law to contractor Walter (Chief) Aiken, had been Collector of Internal Revenue for Atlanta. Other Republican Party leaders included the likes of Henry Lincoln Davis who was quite an orator.

A successor to Henry Lincoln Davis was Benjamin J. Davis, a contractor who built on Auburn Avenue the Odd Fellows Building. His position with the Odd Fellows cemented his high status in the

Black community. The Odd Fellows had the largest hall in the community. Later, Benjamin J. Davis, Jr., became a well-known communist in the '30s and '40s.

In the majority community, there had been progressive voices that made it less difficult for Blacks as they attempted to remove racial barriers. *The Atlanta Constitution*, a newspaper owned by former Governor Cox of Ohio which was bought by him in the 1930s, stood for quiet racial progress. The Commission for Interracial Cooperation, later the Southern Regional Council, was headquartered in Atlanta and made low key, yet determined efforts at breaking down barriers and preventing injustices. An Association of Southern Women Against Lynching performed an even more immediately pressing problem in battling one the most undemocratic remnants of die-hard racism. Lynching was a regular campaign issue of the NAACP which I had joined in the early 1930s and became president of the local chapter in 1939. Of course, in the 1930s and 1940s, former Atlantan, Walter White was Executive Secretary of the National Office.

Around the time of my election to the NAACP presidency, I spoke before the Young Woman's League in West Hunter Baptist Church, in March 1939. I said, "We have no rights in it [American Democracy] that a White man is bound to respect, and it will remain so, as long as the Negro substitutes disorganization for organization..."

In the same speech, I recall speaking against upper-class Black infatuation with tracing their roots to Whites. "We must register and vote, organize and build businesses for the employment of our children and insist upon our rights and fight for them until we win them. There must be no compromise."

My presidency of the NAACP was used vigorously to fight prescriptions laws that were not in the best interest of Blacks. One could say that the NAACP presidency helped to prepare me for direct assault and entrance into politics. I had always had an interest in Political Science. I majored in it during college and thought once of becoming a lawyer, the first profession among professional politics.

In 1957, there was nothing as compelling as an idea whose time had come. Eighty-six years was a long time. No one could accuse Blacks in Atlanta of being impatient. We waited, we worked, we cooperated, and we supported for public office those whom we thought would serve the best interest of all the people. We were not always given a square deal or an equitable distribution of the services of government, but we kept the faith and were encouraged by the fact that in 1953, a Black man, Dr. Rufus Amos, a druggist, and A.T. Walden, a lawyer, were appointed to the Executive Committee of Atlanta which was in charge of the election machinery.

Against this historical backdrop, and with a firm conviction that Atlanta was ready to objectively consider the qualifications of any person, White or Black, who offered for public office, I decided to run for Alderman. It was not a hasty decision. Since 1953, I had expressed my interest in making the effort. As the time drew near to file in 1957, I consulted the leadership of the Black community.

I talked with my friends and with members of my family. My wife and I debated the issue, carefully calculating the risks involved. I had been encouraged by members of my own race and many of my White friends that it was time for a Black to run for the City Administrative Body. I had a few who said that the time was not right and that I wouldn't have a chance.

Certainly, there was danger involved in making such a move at this particular period of increased racial tensions and controversy over civil rights. Some quite frankly said, "A Negro could never win against a White man in a city primary, regardless of qualifications. If he did, they would take the votes away from him, one way or the other."

Whatever the risk and the consequences, I had to know the answer for myself. Furthermore, my children and my children's children should know whether after 86 years, Atlanta had moved to a higher level of municipal equity, racial goodwill and understanding. Nothing can be so thrilling as a risk in a worthy cause backed by faith and hope. It was sometimes more dangerous to avoid a justifiable risk than to take it. There was the possibility of a breakdown of the internal fabric that buttressed our courage and sustained our faith. The time to do what we honestly believed to be right was any time and all the time. It was always expedient and wise to follow an honorable course toward an honorable objective, whatever the consequences may be.

After weighing all the factors, I resolved to run for office. My wife agreed and set the pattern for my campaign before I announced or qualified. She told me, "If you are going to run and have decided it is the thing you should do, I will be with you as I have always been. This I want you to promise: No matter what happens or what is said to you, publicly or privately, you will keep your campaign on the highest possible level and never lower it by striking back or replying to any abuses or insults. Win or lose, you will be respected for the kind of race you ran."

I kept my promise to my wife, and I felt more than a victor because of it. When I told my mother my intentions, she said, very simply and convincingly, "Whatever God wills, it will be done. If it is not what you expected, it will still be His will, so accept it without bitterness or regret. Be careful. I will pray for you as I usually do."

With this, I turned the critical spotlight on myself, my family, my background and experiences. In such an undertaking, it isn't sufficient just to aspire for public office. It is a question of what kind of contribution you can make and why you feel you are the one that should risk involving a whole community in such a speculative and controversial pursuit. If one is honest, his biggest battle is always with himself. One mistake, one unguarded statement, one irresponsible quip in a fit of passion, and the high purposes of the objective, the worthy cause to which I was committed and devoted would be lost, maybe forever.

Thoughtfully, I raised the one pertinent question which I considered all-inclusive: What qualities should a public servant possess? The answers are revealing and while my score was by no means perfect, I thought it passed.

I believed that any person offering for public office should first have a deep and abiding devotion to his community and be interested in the welfare of all the people, indiscriminately, dispassionately, and objectively. This he should have demonstrated in his business enterprises, and served as an officer or director of numerous institutions.

I had worked since 1931 in almost every worthwhile civic and community effort of my city. My wife, my family, and I had shared in all of these experiences with one desire - to be useful, constructive citizens and to help keep Atlanta peaceful, prosperous, and progressive. I had been interested in both the development and the problems affecting my community, and had actively engaged in working out an equitable solution to some of our major difficulties in housing.

I found that the majority of our White citizens were fair and honest in their desire to search for better relations between the races. We talked openly and freely in mutual respect about all of the problems affecting housing and creating racial tensions. We discovered how little we actually knew of the causes or basis for many of the situations which aggravated and strained good racial relations. We found that many of our fears were unfounded and nonexistent. Most of all, we learned to know each other and, in knowing each other, we developed a new concept and a sounder approach to things which sometimes disturbed us and gave us needless sleepless nights.

With relaxed mutual respect and equity, we found the answer to every problem brought before us. Quietly and without fanfare or publicity, we sat many hours during a three-year period, month after month, around a table with leaders of various communities and civic groups of both races, unemotionally and objectively negotiating our differences. Our success was so rewarding that we frequently spent extra time appraising the value and the potential of such a procedure in other areas of mutual concern.

It was in this wholesome community experience that I found a new faith in the innate goodness of the average Southerner. Once we knew the facts and could face them courageously, there was an instinctive and almost passionate desire to be fair. Yes, there were reservations, personal and traditional, but they were usually confined to areas in race relations that were far less significant than those basic problems which were of primary concern to the general welfare and advancement of Blacks to full citizenship and self-respect.

I felt that this experience, more than any other, gave me the courage and hope in offering for public office as Alderman. I humbly believed I could contribute to my city governing body the understanding so much needed at that time. I was confident that many problems with which they were concerned would be alleviated and that much of the pressure under which they operated could be relieved, with a Black man's input.

But when my secret became known that I would run, those with the power raised the registration fee from $300 to $1,000. It was considered too high a price for Blacks to pay. When my former teacher and business associate, L.D. Milton, heard of the move, he said, "Alex, if you've got guts enough to run, I'll be damned if I'm going to let them price you out." And he gave me a $1,000 certified check, and said, "Go up there and register."

With these high purposes in mind, on March 23, 1957, I arrived at the office of the City Executive Committee to pay my $1,000 fee and qualify for Alderman for the Seventh Ward. The office normally opened at 9:00 a.m. I drew place-number-one from the cards on the door. Word spread that a Black was present to qualify for the

Aldermanic race. Things began to hum, and City Hall began to buzz with activity.

By 9:30 a.m., the office was still closed and people were milling in and out of this office, and small groups were spotted through the hall, apparently trying to determine what course of action could be pursued to avoid the action I was about to take. Finally, I got a phone call. City Hall had reached some of the Black leaders and requested that I reconsider in the interest of avoiding injection of racial issues in the campaign. Appeal was made on the basis that if I ran, Dr. Rufus Clement might not be re-elected, and one Black on the Board of Education was better than having none in any branch of city government. A kindly gentleman of another minority group assured me he was "liberal," but my intent to run would affect the mayor's race, and that opponents to the Administration would inject the racial issue and accuse the mayor of influencing me to run. I did not want to hurt the mayor's chance for re-election and yet I could not bring myself to back down.

After some careful thought, I decided that regardless of the consequence, win, lose, or draw, 86 years of "taxation without representation" was long enough to wait. Sooner or later somebody had to find out if the time was right and if Atlanta was ready to rise above the narrow confines of race and ascend to a new and lofty plateau of municipal integrity and national respectability.

I could not wait to see if Atlanta, as a community, would vote "one-16th" representation from one-third of a segment of its population that had not been represented since Reconstruction. Had Atlanta really advanced to this extent? How tall had we grown, in 86 years, above the malarious damps of the lowlands of prejudice and racial discrimination?

I had to have an answer. I had reached the point of no return, and resolutely declared my intention to qualify if the office opened. As soon as my hat hit the political ring, the racial issue became a part of the campaign, but it remained submerged until my victory seemed likely.

With the unanimous endorsement of the Empire Real Estate Board, my determination to run for office was considerably buttressed. The list of my activities in the business world was prominently put forward as evidence of my qualifications for election. In total, I was an executive officer of five firms, and a director of three.

It did not hurt either that Dr. Benjamin E. Mays, in his column, *My View*, said, "He, T.M. Alexander, Sr., is a college graduate and he knows about as much as any Alderman when it comes to the needs of the city, and he has interest in the welfare of all people. Here again, we are fortunate in Atlanta to have a person running for Alderman from the Seventh Ward for whom we can vote without having to say, 'Vote for him because he is a Negro.' " I had the support of most influential Blacks, as well as Black institutions, although at first, some (even Mayor Hartsfield) were concerned for my physical safety.

One never knows what is possible until he ventures forth. I was prepared for whatever would come. I had decided I would speak only to the issues, and not of race. I worked out a platform for better government for all with the following objectives:

1. A sane and equitable tax program. (I had studied the tax structure along with a recent report prepared by a professor at the University of Pennsylvania. I had definite ideas on broadening the tax base with some modifications of our present tax policies.)

2. Carefully planned Slum Clearance and Urban Renewal Program. (We were behind on this program due to various factors which needed study and action.)

3. Improved and adequately compensated police force. (This was under analysis and many of the things I planned to propose were currently the subject of study.)

4. Expansion of city services through wiser use of available or obtainable funds.

5. An accelerated program for attracting new businesses and industries, while stimulating others.

6. Economies of city operations through better businesslike methods.

7. An honest, balanced, and intelligent approach to all civic and community problems.

I truly believed that those seven points were sound and that they represented the major areas with which anyone offering for public office would have to concern himself and take a position. Being new to politics, it did not take long for me to discover how unimportant major issues can be in a political campaign where the real issues were not openly discussed. In my case, the major issue was racial. I could feel it, but I tried to ignore it in my attitude and in my speeches.

In the beginning, I felt very tense and, as accustomed as I was to public speaking, I was obviously nervous at the first all-White rally. I was invited everywhere and accepted all invitations to speak. I attended meetings in every section of the city even though I had been warned that it was unsafe to go into certain sections which were conceded to be antagonistic to Blacks. Somehow, I could not bring myself to believe there was any danger involved, and even if I was not received courteously, or if heckled or booed, I would still retain my poise and cling to my faith. After one of my friends warned me, I told him, "If they won't let me talk, then I'll ask them to let me pray."

Even though I was apprehensive about how I would be received, I was determined to develop no bitterness about the experiences. I could not have been more cordially received anywhere, by anyone, than by the citizens of Atlanta. In every section, every class, and under all circumstances, I was accorded the same, if not superior, treatment as all of the other candidates. This alone justified my faith and effort. There were no insults, no abuse, and I was never ignored nor discriminated against. I conversed freely with the candidates and the voters.

My wife actively campaigned with me and moved freely among the people, and was treated with courtesy and respect on all occasions. They accepted our cards and literature. They shook hands and congratulated me, and openly expressed interest in my speeches which were always "off the cuff" and determined by the inspiration of the audience.

I avoided formal and prepared speeches. At one forum, I perhaps got carried away with the history of Atlanta, so much so, that according to one newspaper, people left the meeting befuddled by my tactic of not mentioning my opponent, and instead showing how much I loved the city by keeping all that statistical information in my head.

Frequently, the other candidates gave me a cue. I studied the reaction of the audience and tried to gear my speeches to fit the occasion. My wife was usually in view and would indicate if she felt I was getting through and whether I should change the pitch of my remarks or not. She could overhear or detect the reaction of those around her.

On one occasion, in a rather critical White community, when I got up to speak, she heard one man remark to another man sitting with him, "Now listen to this colored fellow and compare his speech with the others. He's the best qualified. It's too bad he's a Negro, he'd win without any trouble." On that particular night, a number of speakers had preceded me. I had never heard so many attacks and counterattacks by opponents. There wasn't a kind word said. The audience was obviously bored by criticisms and mud-slinging.

When I was presented, I began by saying, "There is one thing unique about my candidacy. I am probably the only candidate here who isn't mad with anybody, and the person you can vote for who can represent you with peace and with a non-belligerent attitude toward those with whom he will have to work." The audience applauded and my wife smiled and nodded.

I then proceeded to pay high tribute to the character and service of the retiring alderman whom I was seeking to succeed. The audience applauded again. Then, I added, "I'm really not running against anybody. I'm just trying to beat a couple of other fellows to a vacant seat." After my speech, I got a prolonged round of applause. My wife later told me that after my opening statement she heard several persons around her indicate their intention to vote for me. Many did in that precinct, though entirely White.

On another occasion, we attended a political rally in one of the top White communities. Each speaker had one minute after announcing his name and the office for which he was running. I worked a week on a one-minute speech. It was difficult to get the pertinent facts in such a small space. Some candidates ran too short, others had to be rapped down.

When the bell sounded, I was saying, "Thank you." My wife had timed me, over and over, to get the speed and each word exactly in the right place with the right emphasis. One of the candidates met a reporter and one of my assistants outside, and told them that the ovation they heard was "for your boy."

"He just made the best one-minute speech I ever heard."

I am sure I received more comments about this speech than any I made during the campaign.

I had been completely and totally accepted as a "legitimate" candidate for public office by all of my new fellow citizens. My fears and apprehensions left me, and a feeling of belonging and pride in being a full-fledged citizen of respectability inspired my every act. We would stay up each night discussing the pleasant experiences and the various candidates and their families whom we had met. We frequently said that regardless of the out-come of my campaign, the richness of the experience combined with the new faith and hope it inspired, justified the attempt to gain the office.

The feeling we had can best be described by one of our most touching and heart-warming experiences of the whole campaign. Two local civic groups sponsored a parade to "Get Out To Vote." We were invited, as were all other candidates, to participate. All candidates were requested to secure convertible cars. We assembled and were arranged according to the office we sought and the wards from which we were running. As we moved down Peachtree Street, the heart of town, we were all cheered and many kind remarks and good wishes came indiscriminately to my wife, daughter, and me.

As the parade slowed down at one of the intersections, an elderly White woman with beautiful gray hair hanging beneath her sun hat, walked over toward our car and smiling happily, remarked, "Good luck son. Thank God for a new day." I shall never forget that picture nor her statement. Indeed it was a new day, and I, too, thanked God for it. Atlanta had reached a high degree of moral and spiritual maturity. History had not escaped her, nor she it.

Yet having said that, one of the pathetic observations we made in this new, enlightened and encouraging experience was fear of some of our supporters to let their identity be known. I got numerous calls of encouragement from every White community. Some pledged their personal votes for me. Others indicated they were working "quietly" among friends and relatives with whom they felt free to talk. Some stated they favored Blacks having representation in all branches of our Government. Others even suggested that one Black on the Aldermanic Board was inadequate representation for one-third of the population.

The fact that a few Whites knew all of the southern cities that had elected Blacks to their city governing bodies indicated that they had given serious thought to the idea and had reached a logical conclusion. In almost every instance, they prefaced their remarks with, "I'm a native Southerner," and one added, "I suppose my prejudices are as deep as any native Georgian," but he hastily added, "I believe in being fair and just to all people regardless of color."

I listened attentively and courteously whenever I received a call and I told this man who, incidentally, was a minister, "I believe you want to be fair and just, and there are many of your neighbors who feel the same way. You and I know there are more people like you in Atlanta than the other kind. That is why we have a great progressive city." He assured me of his vote and as many of his friends as he could persuade.

Sometimes, I had callers who commended me on my own qualifications and then began criticisms against one or both of my opponents. I usually replied, "I am sure the two gentlemen who are offering for the office to which I aspire feel they are qualified, competent, and worthy also, and because I have only recently met them, I am unable to express an opinion on their qualifications."

My experience and contacts with both of my opponents were most friendly and it would not be an exaggeration to say that our race was the cleanest in the campaign. We did not attack each other, and we strictly adhered to the request of the church people and the papers to avoid the race issue in our campaigning prior to the May 8th Primary Election.

I recall one candidate called me and asked, "How do you think I am doing among your friends?"

I said, "I don't know. How am I doing among yours?"

He replied, "I haven't heard anything. I haven't talked to many of them except about my own race."

"I haven't either," I said.

"How are my opponents doing?"

"I don't know," I answered, and inquired how mine were doing, and he didn't know. Finally, we both laughed and agreed we were about as ignorant as a couple of politicians could be about what was happening.

The race issue was injected one night in another race between a Black and a White candidate for the Board of Education. It was in a community where obviously the White candidate thought it would appeal to the voters. He emphasized that he was "...the only White man running against the one Negro member of the Board of Education." When he made the statement, there was a freezing resentment that engulfed the entire audience, all of whom were White. When he finished, the applause was extremely light, just a courteous clap of a few hands and audible mumbling of disapproval. The Black opponent's applause was thunderous.

When my wife and I were leaving the building after the rally, a middle-aged White woman stopped us and said, "Mr. and Mrs. Alexander, I would like to apologize for that man. We don't approve of his statement." With tears of regret and shame in her eyes, and holding us both by the arm, she added, "For the first time in my life, I feel almost ashamed that I'm a member of the White race."

We knew too well the feeling of shame, sorrow, and of regret. Surely, we had more experience with this type of thing than she, and we knew her hurt was great.

A few days before the close of the campaign, a man called me and when he told me where he lived, I knew he was White. He said he wanted to help me and asked if he could come to my office the next day. I told him the address and we agreed on the time. He came and I was in my private office. I heard him inquire for me, and I went out to meet him. When I got to the outer office, he had stopped and was gazing around like he was lost or amazed at something. I almost immediately detected the situation and rushed to him, shook his hand, and introduced myself.

He looked at me, still puzzled and silent, and finally said, "Are you the one running for Alderman?"

I said, "Yes, I am," half leading him to the privacy of my office and away from my staff who had abandoned work to observe his behavior. He seemed reluctant until I said, "Come back here, I want to tell you something privately." When I got him comfortably seated and a little relaxed, I pulled my chair close to the end of my desk where he was seated and came straight to the point. Looking him squarely in the eye, pleasantly, I inquired, "You didn't know I was a Negro candidate, did you?"

He smiled and said with not too much embarrassment, "No, I sure didn't."

I firmly believe that all of the experiences which life sends us have a hidden blessing. Like Jacob, I was determined to try to wrestle one out of this situation. It was a challenge and an opportunity to test my power of persuasion. Every vote counts, and I particularly wanted this one.

I told him how long I had lived and worked in the community, about my family, my business, and civic connections. I sighted some incidents with which I was sure he was familiar relative to the bombing of some houses in a tense area. I told him how, through getting together around a table, the good citizens of both races had settled the matter. I named prominent citizens whom he knew and told him to check what I was telling him about my qualifications and my service to the community. He listened attentively without saying a word. He seemed in deep concentration on my every word. I did not know whether I was getting through favorably or not.

I pulled out all the stops. I recited all I could think of about the city. I took every issue and gave my views and what I thought I could contribute to the solution of the major problems confronting us. I assured him that a number of White people were supporting me and some particular ones were openly campaigning for me. Then I sat back to get the verdict.

He said, "I think you will make a good representative and I would like to help you but I don't know how I could, because I don't know what the people in my neighborhood would think if I asked them to vote for a colored man." He got up to leave and paused, as if debating something in his own mind. Then he turned, looking at me, and said, "But I sure would like to see you win." Suddenly, as though he had to answer, he added, "The folks in my neighborhood don't know you are colored either. Give me some of your cards, without your picture - damned if I'm going to tell them."

He wished me luck and shook my hand warmly as he left with a pocketful of cards, without my picture. After he had gone, my sorrow for him subordinated what appeared to have been a victory. We were both in search of freedom and we would have to find it together or not at all. Can lying by negation lead to truth? Or, can truth denied lead to freedom? As we sought the answer to our common problem, such experiences confounded, confused, and perplexed us. I would like to have believed his vote was among those from his precinct. If so, he was one step closer to the answer, for at least his mind was free, though in secret.

On May 7th, the final rally was held at a large Black church. All of the candidates were present. This concluded my thirtieth meeting. The church was packed with Whites and Blacks. I was glad this was the end. It had been a hard-fought battle but free from racial animosity and mudslinging. All in all, it was a well-disciplined campaign and I had no regrets that I had ventured into this new experience.

The constant drive night after night had taken its toll, causing me to drop only five pounds in the ordeal. I welcomed the release of tension. I would miss the speeches, the debates, the charges, and counter charges, the elements of surprise we always looked for.

There had evolved a sort of mutual respect and goodwill between my opponents and me that evoked commendations from other candidates. One night, one of my opponents and I were standing by a table talking, and he was helping me fold my campaign cards. Another candidate came up and said, "Now, I have seen everything. Are you running against each other or together?"

We let him in on what we were talking about. We had just remarked how much we had enjoyed knowing each other and our regret that we happened to turn up as opponents. We also had committed ourselves to continue our friendship regardless of the outcome of the race and pledged that if either one of us won, we would try to be a good representative for the other. This was the spirit which existed between the three of us. Now, on this final night, the impact of all those experiences made me everything but political minded.

When it came my time to speak, I was obviously choked with emotions. It was like the final day of graduation when old friends have to part. The unity and pride engendered among my own people and their support and loyalty were unprecedented. I had carried a heavy load up a steep and treacherous hill, moving cautiously but forward. I had not let them down and they were pleased over the character of the battle I had waged, not just for a Black but for all the good citizens of our community. I finally began my speech after a loud round of applause which made it even more difficult:

"My friends and neighbors. I don't feel political-minded tonight. I just want to thank all of you for the contribution you have made, in numerous ways, to my campaign. As I said in the beginning, I am but a symbol of your voice. I've tried to be worthy of your confidence. I have not embarrassed you. I have kept my campaign on the high level representative of your hopes, your dreams, and your aspirations. I want to pay tribute to the other candidates, including my opponents, for the cordial and congenial way in which we have been received all over the city. Not once have we had occasion to feel mistreated or unwelcome wherever we went. Now, may I present my real manager, my wife, who has gone through this experience with me as she has all of my experiences for twenty-five years. This week she was nominated as *Mother of the Year* from Georgia to the National Body of Mothers."

My wife stood up in the rear to acknowledge the applause of the crowd. She was seated between the wives of two other candidates.

This was a sad occasion for her, too, for we both made many friends.

I concluded, "Now I have done my best. The experience has been worth the effort. I now leave it where I began - the will of the Lord and the vote of His people."

I had finished and I was prepared for victory or defeat with complete peace of mind. During the entire campaign I had not had a sleepless night. I tried to think of myself as the instrument of my people who, for 86 years, had been without a representative. I was not running as a person, I was simply a symbol, and I felt honored and humbled to be used in so great a cause.

May 8th was a beautiful sunshiny spring day. Enthusiasm was high, and the voting was heavy as had been predicted by the press. The Mayor's campaign was conceded to vie for top interest with the Board of Education. It had also been concluded by most politicians that in my three-cornered race, I would emerge as one of the contenders in a "run-off." I had hoped for a miracle, but short of that, practical politics validated their conclusion and I felt that was the worst that could happen to me as we projected our voting strength.

We set up headquarters for getting the returns at my home. Poll watchers were dispatched to each of the 71 voting precincts. The polls closed at 8:00 p.m., and from then, we were tabulating returns as they came over the phone in rapid succession. The race narrowed down early to a two-way battle with the third man moving out of the picture. It was neck-and-neck, first one, and then the other took the lead, though never by a great margin.

When the final count was in, my opponents had 27,993 and 14,052 votes, respectively, and I had polled 22,836. Neither had a clear majority and I had been forced into the "run-off" for May 22nd, two weeks later. Our ward was 65 percent White and 35 percent Black, and my top opponent beat me by 1,600 votes in our ward.

All of the Black voters did not vote for me, nor did all the Whites vote for my opponent. I had substantial White support and the majority of Black support. Had every Black voted for me who was qualified to vote, I still could not have had a clear majority in a three-man race. I considered the "run-off" a victory and was encouraged by the number of White citizens who voted for me.

The next two weeks would be a difficult kind of campaign. There were two other positions that would have to be settled in the "run-off." There would be no rallies, but a lot of foot work and contacts by mail and phone. Atlanta had been to the polls twice - once for the Bond issue in April and the Primary on May 8th. Now they were asked to go to another election.

The history of "run-off" elections showed that the voting was always extremely light. The problem was to stimulate enough interest to get out a large vote. My job was to get the 22,000 back. It was generally agreed that I could win if I got 15,000 Black voters back along with 50 percent of my White support. We set out to get all of the Black voters back and felt confident that the stimulus of the primary results would give them some reassurance that victory was possible. Unless there was an unusual situation, fewer White voters return to the polls in a run-off; statistics bore this out.

The closer we came to May 22nd, the more confident we became of winning. The odds were two-to-one in my favor. I avoided overconfidence because I knew this was unprecedented and I expected a heavier vote than normal, but I felt that I could win with 20,000. I was not alone in this conviction, as was subsequently borne out.

However, lightning had not yet struck. On May 17, around 4:30 p.m., I received a call at my office from one of the news services. I was apprehensive and amazed when the reporter asked, "Have you heard the Governor's statement about you?"

I said, "No, what kind of statement?"

"Let me read it to you," he replied. As he read, something deep inside of me seemed to die. I felt like I was being choked by an invisible relentless hand, but I suddenly re-gathered my strength and braced myself. He read from portions of the article in the newspaper:

GOVERNOR GRIFFIN URGES ATLANTA
TO VOTE AGAINST NEGRO

In calling for the nomination of Jack Summers as Alderman from the 7th ward, Griffin said, "...It is high time that the White voters of Atlanta did some bloc voting themselves. It is not my policy to interfere, at any time, in the political affairs of the City of Atlanta or any other municipality or local government. However, I feel that the result of the aldermanic race is so important to the people of the entire State that I have no hesitancy in calling on my friends and all the friends of segregation to support Mr. Summers in this race.

"...Mr. Summers is a well-informed man who is in complete sympathy with the preservation of the traditions and customs of the Southern people. It is no time to elect a Negro Alderman, at this critical period in our affairs. We are on the verge of developments in Atlanta and the rest of Georgia relative to segregation in our schools and other concomitant fields which makes it a paramount necessity for the voters of Atlanta to elect a White man in this race. You may be sure the Negroes will vote virtually as a unit. It is the duty of every true patriot in Atlanta, to lay aside all business, if necessary, and go to the polls to see that Summers is elected."

I was asked for my comment for the press. I just said what I felt and refused to elaborate on it at any time. This was the statement as made then and never added to or changed in any way:

"Governor Griffin has a right to his opinion and Atlanta has a right to make its choice. The will of the Lord will be voiced by the people

Wednesday. Thirty-eight percent of Atlanta's population is Negro. I am only asking for one-sixteenth voice on the Aldermanic Board. I have kept my campaign on a high plane and I hope to keep it there. Whatever is said, I don't plan to strike back."

I had not calculated this type of thing. No one had. This was the first open injection of the race issue and the appeal to prejudice. I was not prepared for such an unprecedented move. Time was running out. I would have to come down to a plateau too low to live with myself, face my people or be fit for public office if I retaliated in kind. If I couldn't win with respect, I would rather lose than fight in the lowlands of racial hate and prejudice. My objective was not to create problems and ill will, but instead, to help solve them through cooperation and goodwill.

As soon as the news hit the papers, radio, and television, my phone rang until midnight every day up through the May 22nd. The resentment to the Governor's statement seemed unusually large, and the good people of Atlanta and Georgia were indignant and ashamed. It was predicted on every hand that it would boomerang and rebound to my favor and election. Letters literally poured in and many contained small or substantial contributions. What we mostly appreciated were the sentiments of encouragement and hope.

One White lady called and said, "I didn't vote for you before, but I am this time. You are a gentleman and I want you to win."

Another said, "I vote under extreme handicap, I have a young baby and my husband works for a department of the State, but I want you to know that all the White people do not feel as our Governor does, and my husband and I are going to vote for you again."

Dozens pledged the votes of their families and all the friends they could get to the polls. Some used their cars to carry people who could not get to the polls.

It appeared that the Governor's statement was having the reverse effect. Blacks were resolved to go all out for their full voting strength and as a result, a program was set up to solicit 1,000 persons to commit themselves to get twenty-two individuals to the polls.

The White press took no position editorially. Instead, they printed letters and statements to the editors protesting the Governor's interference in a local election. The Black press attempted, editorially, to create an atmosphere of active retaliation and appealed to the better citizens to decide the issue on merit and qualifications of the candidates.

The identity of race in the press, up to the Governor's statement, was not emphasized by the reporters. Neither did the radio or television programs play up the race issue. On the other hand, from May 17 to May 22, in all three media, the fact that I was a Black and that I was running against a White man was continuously repeated. My picture, the Governor's, and my opponents' were flashed on the television screens with practically every review of the news.

The Governor's statement was read and re-read. *This is the First Time Since Reconstruction a Negro has Run for Alderman* was a headline in article after article. Neighborhood newspapers appealed for votes against me, purely on the basis of my racial identity. One paper, apologetically, commended me on my race and said that I was a credit to the Negro race and the city, but they endorsed my opponent stating it was not because I was a Negro.

In spite of this constant barrage of opposition and attack, I still held fast because letters were still coming as were the encouraging telephone calls. I began to feel that the good people of Atlanta rose up with righteous indignation and were saying to the world, "Atlanta is an oasis of peace, goodwill, and democracy in the South."

The 22nd of May came. My family and I went to cast our vote. At 11:30 a.m. there was a constant stream of old and young voters. I was told that one man was carried from his sick bed on a stretcher to cast his vote. The press took pictures of us and the lines of Blacks at the polls. This was destined to be the biggest turnout of voters in a run-off in the history of Atlanta. At noon, it was obvious that Blacks were voting in larger numbers than Whites.

It was estimated by those visiting the polls that I was in the lead, two-to-one. My lead was still holding steady at 2:00 p.m. Then the radio and television stations starting playing up the news, flashing the pictures over the air, and announcing that Negroes were out-voting the Whites two-to-one. This kept up until the polls closed.

When the count was in, I had polled 22,459 to my opponent's 32,170, and the vote was nearly 55,000 for a new record in a run-off election. My opponent had won by 9,711 votes. In the other run-off between two White candidates, the votes cast for the two were 48,934 or 6,695 fewer votes than in our contest. There were at least that number of voters who went specifically to vote in only one of the races.

It was alleged, and many persons validated it who were witnesses, that I actually lost the race after 2:00 p.m. After the radio and television appeals to White voters apparently failed, trucks, cars, and buses were employed, a battery of telephones used, and workers were sent house to house to get Whites to the polls. People were lured out of their homes and picked up at work and escorted to the polls with the one cry, "Come on and vote - that nigger is winning."

Some had estimated the cost to the opposition to defeat me as high as $62,000. These and many other reports came to me, but whatever the truth was, I had absolutely no bitterness in my heart and nor did I love my city less.

After the election, more letters came from all over the state and every section of the country. I did not realize how a non-victor could be made to feel so much like a victor. I guess I was so concerned with the cause that I lost sight of what good could come from defeat. Blacks in the South knew it was possible to run for public office in the land of our forebears and do it with dignity and poise on an equal basis. The Blacks in Atlanta knew, regardless of our failure in the first effort,

Griffin Urges Atlanta To Vote Against Negro

By WILLIAM M. BATES

Gov. Griffin Friday publicly entered Atlanta's city runoff campaign by urging white voters to defeat a Negro candidate for the Board of Aldermen in Wednesday's second primary.

In calling for the nomination of Jack Summers as alderman from the 7th Ward, Griffin said: "It is high time that the white voters of Atlanta did some 'bloc voting' themselves."

Summers, a barber supply salesman, led a field of three in last week's city primary but failed to obtain a majority.

The runner-up in the first primary and Summers' opponent in Wednesday's run-off is T. M. Alexander, prominent Negro insurance company executive.

Griffin, in a move virtually unprecedented in recent Georgia politics, issued a public statement endorsing Summers as a "well-informed man who is in complete sympathy with the preservation of the traditions and customs of the Southern people."

"It is not my policy to interfere, at any time, in the political affairs of the City of Atlanta or any other municipality or local government," Griffin declared.

"However, I feel that the result of this aldermanic race is so important to the people of the entire state that I have no hesitancy in calling on my friends and all friends of segregation to support

Continued on Page 2, Column 6

Don't Vote For Negro, Griffin Ask

Continued From Page

Mr. Summers in this race," he said.

Summers, who bears a striking resemblance to the late Eugene Talmadge, visited Griffin's office shortly before the first primary. Griffin made no comment prior to that contest.

Mayor Hartsfield, who was renominated in last week's voting, issued the following statement:

"I think this matter can be left to the good judgement of the voters of Atlanta."

He declined to elaborate.

HAS A RIGHT

Alexander declared that Griffin "has a right to his opinion and Atlanta has a right to make its choice." He said the "will of the Lord will be voiced by the people of Atlanta Wednesday."

"Thirty-eight per cent of Atlanta's population is Negro and I'm only asking for one-sixteenth voice on the aldermanic Board," Alexander said.

"I have kept my campaign on a high plane and I hope to keep it there," he added. "Whatever is said I don't plan to strike back."

In his prepared statement, Griffin said "it is no time" to elect a Negro alderman "at this critical period in our affairs."

SCHOOL SEGREGATION

"We are on the verge of developments in Atlanta and the rest of Georgia relative to segregation in our schools and other concomitant fields which makes it a paramount necessity for the voters of Atlanta to elect a white man in this race," the governor stated.

"It is high time that the white voters of Atlanta did some 'bloc voting' themselves," he said. "You may be sure that the Negroes will vote virtually as a unit."

"It is the duty of every true patriot in Atlanta to lay aside all business, if necessary, and go to the polls to see that Summers is elected."

In last week's balloting, Summers polled 27,993 votes against 22,836 for Alexander. A third candidate, Lanier Randall, received 14,052 votes and was eliminated from the run-off.

Dr. Rufus Clement, a Negro member of the city board of Education, was elected to a second term last week in a two-man race against a white challenger

This article appeared in the *Atlanta Constitution* newspaper on May 17, 1957 during the City Board of Alderman's race.

Vote For

T. M. ALEXANDER

REPUBLICAN CANDIDATE

STATE SENATOR
38th District

NOVEMBER 6th

1961 Campaign
brochure
during T.M.'s run
for the
Georgia State
Senate.

A VOTE ALL CITIZENS WILL BE

PROUD TO CAST

B
E
C
A
U
S
E

that it was not an impossibility. We knew, too, that our city had moved forward and that there were White people who would look objectively and without prejudice at a Black candidate and listen to him with equal courtesy and respect.

The White citizens of Atlanta had experienced something new as well and could now subject themselves to an honest appraisal of the progress made in race relations. They could see how important it was not to take progress for granted in a growing metropolitan city. Much of our trouble was "underground" and subtle. Subsequently, we felt that whatever lurked hidden and suppressed could not be allowed to create a climate that would bring it out into the open. For instance, all of the goodwill generated in the campaign, including its freedom from race-bating tactics, could have all been destroyed had the good citizens not openly revolted over the precedent set by the chief executive of our state.

The first and only threatening call and the only abuse to which I was subject was 24 hours following the Governor's appeal. At 3:20 a.m., I was called and subjected to the most violently abusive language and threats imaginable. I remained calm and was not afraid. I restrained my anger, which was not too easy to do at 3:20 a.m.

After this failed exhilarating try for the City Board of Alderman, I ventured out again in electoral politics in 1961, this time to run for the Georgia State Senate. My statement of candidacy read as follows:

STATEMENT OF T.M. ALEXANDER, SR.
CANDIDATE FOR STATE SENATOR,
38TH SENATORIAL DISTRICT OF GEORGIA

"My candidacy is based on the hope that the people of the Thirty-eighth District and Fulton County will see fit to use my 31 years experience in business, civic, religious, and political affairs to strengthen representative government in my great state. For too long a time, Georgians have been denied the stimulus and inspiration of truly representative government.

"As a consequence, the people of the new Thirty-eighth District have not only been neglected by the Georgia Legislature but, more importantly, we have not been allowed to contribute fully to the progress and glory of Georgia. As the elected representative of my district, I hope not only to represent our needs but also our talents, our ideas, and our loyalty.

"I am proud to be running as a Republican in what has always been known as a one-party state. It is my firm belief that truly representative government is impossible without the competition of two parties, each of which can control the direction and quality of the other. My election as a Republican will do much to shatter the indifference of the state and the nation toward people who cannot have their desires and needs recognized because of the lack of free expression between two competitive political philosophies.

"I solicit the vote and support of all citizens of the Thirty-eighth District and Fulton County in the primary and the general elections. Together, we can move Georgia forward to her destined potential as the greatest industrial, educational, and agricultural state in the nation. To these lofty ends, with God's help and your support, I solemnly dedicate myself to the service of Georgia and the people of my district."

Leroy Johnson was elected to the State Legislature, and he became the first Black to hold this position since Reconstruction days. This election attracted nationwide attention. I remember the Boston Globe did a story on it. In a sense, a good result came of my initial try in 1957.

In the midst of this race, however, my mother died and was buried from Dexter Avenue Church. And less than a year later, my father also passed; he was buried from the church where he had served as Chairman of the Trustee Board. He had never been confined until two weeks before his death, at which time he said he "wanted to join Hattie." This period in my life was one of the saddest.

Urban Renewal or
Negro Removal

*When you've got your hands in the lion's mouth, don't
tickle his tonsils.*

T.M. Alexander, Sr.

In our efforts to gain a foothold in decent housing, there were
successes in the early 1950s. However, it remained a continuous
struggle. By the late 1950s, slums still existed in Atlanta as elsewhere
in the nation. Urban renewal (or was it Negro Removal?) was on
everybody's lips. I was called upon to speak several times on this
issue.

Just having run for public office, I had a certain rapport and
"entre" greater than in the past with which to say the things I wanted
said.

I was the keynote speaker on the issue of urban renewal before a
regional housing meeting on November 14, 1957. On this occasion,
I said:

"Mr. Chairman, distinguished guests, members of the
Empire Real Estate Board, members of the University system,
and visiting friends:

"We are privileged to welcome you here to share in the experiences of a two-day housing clinic on urban renewal, which is jointly sponsored by the Atlanta Empire Real Estate Board and the Atlanta University Center. This occasion, unique in its sponsorship, is indicative of the type of cooperation and coordination which exists between our educational institutions and the business and professional groups of our community on all matters which involve or affect the welfare, the progress, the peace, and the security of all the people of our great city. Such cooperation of all segments of a growing city, the exchange of points of views, the combination of skills and know-how for the common good, is the hallmark and genius which made and keeps Atlanta the peaceful, prosperous, and progressive city in which we take justifiable pride.

"So, we invited you here because we modestly believe that Atlanta more nearly represents, in the South, a sense of direction, so essential to keeping on a true course, and evolving a pattern of community cooperation which is indispensable to the growth and development of the South. We invited you here, too, because we are, have been, and will continue to be a potent and effective part of the history and economic progress of the South. We have a contribution in its past, a vested interest in its present, a coveted stake in the future! Therefore, we are committed to share its responsibilities and problems as citizens and equally enjoy the benefits of success which are inherent in its future...

"As a result of this meeting, we hope not only will there be a clearer understanding of the program, but wider participation and concern. We further expect to arrive at a solution to some of the problems already apparent and which threaten to bog down the program unless solved expeditiously and equitably.

"We hope and urge that those of you from other cities throughout the country, and particularly the South, will be inspired and encouraged to organize the leadership in your communities; that you may understand, interpret, participate in and benefit by all that Urban Renewal is intended to accomplish.

"If we can accomplish the high objectives of this Clinic on Urban Renewal, every American citizen will be adequately housed and our great cities will be unimpaired by slums and blight, and we shall have reached a new plateau of community cooperation and goodwill for the common good.

"It is then not amiss to conceive that history may record that Urban Renewal, a new and broad concept of housing, rehabilitation, and slum clearance, became the architect for not only the rebuilding of American cities, but exemplified, the faith and spirit of cooperation so essential to good government and the mutual progress of all citizens."

Some four months later, I represented the particular concerns of local Blacks before elected officials regarding urban renewal. I spoke specifically upon the *Atlanta Urban Renewal Program*, a study offered by officials. I said:

". . . It should be clearly understood and emphasized that we are for slum clearance and urban renewal in the City of Atlanta. We will support in general, the overall objectives of such a program provided it is carried out according to the spirit and intent of Congress, with one of the specific objectives being the removal of the impact of slums and blight from human lives. Our studies show that the removal of slums and blight leads to a sharp and often amazing reduction in crime and disease and the corresponding need for corrective municipal services, and to a tremendous increase in tax return from such areas when they have been restored to productive use.

"There is no question that Black families in Atlanta, as elsewhere in the country, constitute a disproportionately high percentage of the families which occupy the areas affected by the urban renewal and slum clearance projects. It would seem, therefore, to be a natural consequence that they would constitute majority shareholders in the benefits derived from the program. Our considerations show, however, that slum clearance and urban re-development programs, while affording substantial benefits to minority groups if they are fairly administered, are also laden with potential risks to minority families. There are restrictions inherent in the Atlanta program which are an immediate threat to our housing conditions, and the extent to which we are restricted governs the degree to which our housing condition could be damaged. Therefore, the risks, the complications, and the difficulties with which we are faced in attempting to achieve sound and acceptable relocation of Atlanta's Urban Renewal Program are a basic part of our grave concern."

At other times, I was involved in the rather detailed negotiations over specifics. These were the kinds of things I could do well, having dealt with figures, percentages, and bottom line as an insurance executive.

I suppose one of my most willing spokesman's role took place with regard to urban renewal-revitalization of the Butler Street area around the YMCA, on June 12, 1959 to the Board and the Citizens Committee on Urban Renewal:

". . . When rights are thoroughly understood, properly guaranteed, and adequately protected, the American people of all races, colors, and creeds, in all areas of our nation, can be depended upon to live up to the principles of democracy with due respect to their neighbors, and strive to live in peace and happiness. We therefore recommend:

I. That a Commission on Democracy in Housing be appointed by the President of the United States to study the problems nationally and locally where Federal funds are involved and make recommendations to the proper officials, organizations, and citizens involved whereby similar state and local commissions be encourage to ensure local participation.

II. That local, state, and national legislative bodies be called upon to pass legislation which assures the rights of freedom of choice, open occupancy, and quiet enjoyment. Adequate provisions should be made for the establishment and promotion of good public relations, especially at local levels.

III. That all laws and regulations involving the expenditure of Federal funds provide for the maintenance of these three rights for each citizen in every area of our nation, otherwise such Federal funds will not be committed to the projects involved.

IV. That you recommend to the President, the Congress, and the Department of Justice, the enactment of laws and regulations which will provide for the investigation, prosecution, and assessment of damages for acts of violence and denials of rights or in respect to projects where the expenditure of Federal funds is involved.

V. That where the expenditure of Federal funds on projects such as schools, highways, government installations, or other national or interstate projects requiring the displacement of families, laws and regulations be enacted to require plans for adequate relocation of such families before the expenditure of Federal funds can be approved."

But, while considering adequate housing for Blacks as my civic duty, I also approached housing from a business standpoint. When my father retired and the construction business became more mechanized, my brother and I organized a construction firm in Atlanta that I incorporated, with an accountant, foreman, and proper machinery. We did very well. My brother handled the day-to-day field operations. I handled the accounting and finance. We were headed for a successful business when my mother became ill and my father was in his 80s.

I could not leave Atlanta since I had responsibility for three corporations, Southeast Fidelity Insurance Company, Security Construction, and the real estate firm of Alexander & Calloway. My operations constituted a small conglomerate, long before that term for diversification became popular.

Nothing was more important than the welfare of my parents, therefore, I suggested to my brother, Julius, that he go back to Montgomery and help look after mamma and papa. Both my sisters were married and away from Montgomery. I agreed to finish the jobs in process.

I struggled vainly to maintain the business, but it proved to be too much for me. I had stretched myself too thinly. I was being cheated, abused, and generally taken advantage of. I lost $40,000. The bonding company I indemnified with my assets paid the debts. However, I was advised to bankrupt the corporation and myself. Then, I remembered what papa said about your word being your bond. I decided that I would repay the bonding company. This I immediately began to do as rapidly as I could.

The manager of the company in Atlanta knew I had been taken advantage of by two White lawyers who had done construction for me and two Blacks ones also, who were not willing to assume part of the overruns due to changes they made in the contracts without written change orders.

We asked the bonding company to reduce my obligation, which they did. I, in turn, wrote the company a letter commending their Atlanta manager and his cooperation and what an asset he was to their business. He later got a promotion.

Eventually, I finished all the jobs, at no extra cost to the owners, paid all bills and obligations, and then closed down the company. At the same time, W.L. Calloway and I were doing well in real estate and insurance and shared some of the losses. No one suffered but us. We retained credibility and continued our other businesses.

To recoup our losses, we did two things. I took a long-term capital loss against income, upon the advice of my lawyer and friend, who had become an attorney in the Treasury Department of the Government. Then Calloway and I bid on a piece of city property between Anderson Avenue and West Lake Drive, now known as Calloway Drive. With a mutual friend, A.V. Jett, we developed that subdivision and made a profit from the land and sale of the houses.

Calloway and I were both charter members of the National Association of Realtors, which we set up with the help of Maceo Smith at a Tampa, Florida, meeting. We remained active in the real estate and insurance businesses which complemented and supplemented each other. He was oriented to real estate, and I to insurance.

With the guidance and assistance of my great friend and mentor, John Sibley, Sr., I had been able to secure the necessary financial assistance to develop a semi-luxury apartment complex of a 127 unit apartment in the midst of the Atlanta University facility at the overall cost of more than $1.3 million in urban renewal land. I had to bid on the 5.27 acres.

Again, I remembered something my father said, "Never bid in round figures on anything. Twenty-five cents can be the difference between the high and low bid. " So I bid $127,250.25 to construct two buildings which had to give the illusion of being two circles. (We used panels that gradually made the circles). After a civic meeting dealing with the destruction of a wall that had been constructed across a main street to separate the White and expanding Black community, I won the bid. I was assigned lawyer Hamilton Douglas to guide me legally. Financing was arranged through Adams-Cates and Metropolitan Life for $800,000 at 6 percent.

When the costs ran about $375,000 above the first mortgage to build, furnish, and landscape the grounds, several banks placed funds in the Trust Company Bank and made me a second mortgage loan at 5 1/2 percent to avoid Metropolitan's increase to 7 percent for the additional money needed.

I had never done a development of this size and did not want to risk losing the money of my friends. So, my son T.M. Jr., Manager Harold Dawson, and my son's father-in-law, Dr. Hilliard Bowen, and I put $50,000 up front while my White friends furnished the remainder. My integrity and reputation were on the line. There was no room for error or mismanagement. This was a test and a chance to break through and prove we had what it took to help develop Atlanta and make a contribution to its inevitable growth and progress.

My word was my bond, and it was a total success. In the end, everybody profited, no money was lost, and all debts were paid. The apartments were owned by Clark College, and stood as testimony to Black credibility and integrity.

My next opportunity followed with the same friends with whom I had established myself. They acquired for me some 50 acres of undeveloped land, now known as Harris Manor, off Peyton Road. We borrowed the money to subdivide the land, cut streets, and put in any additions required. We sold lots to a developer and repaid the money as we sold the lots to the group, headed by Sibley.

When the project was completed, I carried Sibley in my car to see this beautiful community of brick homes, totalling in excess of $3 million, added to the tax digest of the city. Again, all obligations were paid, no loss to anyone.

Later, I was called in by Sibley and told that their organization had acquired, through a White woman broker, a large tract of land on the other side of Utaw Creek which crossed Peyton Road, stretching toward the Cascade area, and populated by predominantly White middle class neighborhoods.

He said, "We like what you have done, and we want to be sure that there is nothing limiting to normal expansion and growth of our city, to the benefit of all our citizens. We don't want you to have to pay taxes on this land, so we will keep it in our name, and save it until you are ready to do some further development. And, as is the custom of Southerners in their relationship with those they respect and trust, nothing is hidden. "We paid," he said, $2,500 an acre. We will hold it for you and sell it to you at $3,000 an acre, whenever you are ready."

Because of extensive construction going on, at times there were costly delays, especially when you are operating with borrowed money. Knowing this, my partner and I decided to take a breather from dealing with City Hall on getting land improvements. Therefore, I didn't immediately purchase the land from Sibley.

However, a contractor who had worked to the satisfaction of me and my friends in the Harris Manor deal wanted to develop the land offered to me by Sibley. But at the time, he didn't know who owned it, which led him down to City Hall to find out who the owners were.

He discovered that they were the same ones who financed me on the 50-odd acres he developed for us at Harris Manor. He went to my friends and asked to buy the land. John Sibley told him it belonged to me. He said, "But it's not in Alexander's name."

"Yes, but it's promised to him and only if he agrees to sell it to you can you get it." He discussed no price, but came back to me and explained what happened and asked me if I would allow him to buy it. I asked him how much was he willing to pay per acre. He said, "$3,500." That was $500 more an acre than I had been promised I could buy it for!

I told him, "Let me think about it and I will let you know if I want to buy and keep it for a while." I could not pay cash for the land and wanted no longer to try to develop housing at this period. I needed time to get back to Sibley.

I could have managed a deal like this, using a contract from the buyer as collateral for a loan. However, I had no need or inclination to pull a trick on people who had done so much for me and who were able to risk large sums of money in worthy causes from which I benefited. It never crossed my mind to do other than go back to Sibley, tell him the whole story and release him from the promise to sell to me first. This was proof of my commitment to honesty.

I told Sibley that his group could make an extra $500 per acre by selling it directly to the development contractor and I expressed my confidence in his ability to do a job as good or better than he had done for us on Harris Manor.

He looked at me in his soft, smiling eyes, showing obvious satisfaction. "Alexander," he said, "the people I represent don't need to make any more money." Knowing those he represented, I knew that if I walked across the street and bought anything in Atlanta, they made some money. He continued, "You have been fair to us and we want to be fair to you. If you don't have the money to buy the land, go downstairs (I was in Trust Company Bank) and tell so-and-so I said let you have the money you need to get this land in your name, record it, and transfer it to the developer at $3,500 an acre; pay us the $3,000 we promised to sell it to you for, repay the loan, and make yourself and your associate the $500 an acre." This I did and invested not one dollar of personal money.

I enjoyed a lasting friendship with John Sibley and his associates. I had their respect and their goodwill, a relationship that had sustained me. I had tried to live up to the legacy of my parents: Your word is your bond.

I never sued or had been sued, nor faulted on a debt, never wrote a bad check or forgot my mama's proverb, "You can't hit a straight lick with a crooked stick," and I never lost what I got by the right method.

Finally, with regard to providing decent housing dwellings for Blacks prior to 1963, and prior to public accommodation laws, a group of visitors being shown through the Black residential and business sections of Atlanta were awed, and expressed great surprise that here in the South such progress had been made in minority group housing. They were equally amazed at the large number of Black businesses, and particularly of the strength and soundless of Black financial institutions. They were overwhelmed as they viewed the vast private educational combine which made Atlanta the "Black Educational Capital of America." It was easily conceded that no city equaled Atlanta for economic progress among its Black citizens.

One by one, the group popped the question.

"How did you people accomplish this?"

"What are the sources of income for Blacks in Atlanta? How did you get the money to develop these beautiful communities?"

One ventured to admit, "I had heard about it, but I would have never believe this existed if I did not see it. How do Blacks and Whites in Atlanta get along?"

The questions were coming so fast and furious that there was not enough time to answer them adequately in the period of the tour. This type of situation was frequent in Atlanta where many Blacks from all over the country came to see first-hand what the native Black population so proudly proclaimed as they traveled throughout the country.

The Texan had nothing on the Black Atlantan in public relations. An Atlanta Black was literally a "Walking Chamber of Commerce."

North, South, East, and West, or abroad, the word spread that "Atlanta is the oasis of the South. It's different and there is no place like it!" I felt this was a realistic comparison not only with other southern cities but with cities throughout the country.

The Struggle -
Obstacles Surpassed

Retribution is as sharp sighted as Justice is blind.
                                    T.M. Alexander, Sr.

> **In** 1957, my efforts to get elected to the Board of Alderman took place in the midst of great unrest in southern Black communities. The greatest amount of racial change was being led by Dr. Martin Luther King, Jr., in Montgomery, Alabama. There, he was pastor of Dexter Avenue Baptist, my old home church. I had known the King family for years. Martin Luther King, Sr., married me and my wife in the basement of the church. All in all, we had good relations.

When Martin, Jr., was a student at Morehouse, I was frequently called upon, as a former varsity debater, as one of the judges for oratorical contests in which he participated. I saw him grow in stature and wisdom, and thought he was going to be a lawyer. When he decided to go into the ministry, Martin Luther, Sr., wisely told him, "Don't do it unless you just can't help yourself." He could not have done otherwise because the mantle of his grandfather and his father had fallen on him, and he was chosen and destined for greatness.

I made frequent trips to Montgomery during my parents' life-times, and always taught my mother's Sunday School class on Mother's Day. Over the years, Dexter had withstood every attempt to be removed from Main Street which was one block from the capitol and surrounded on all sides by state buildings. For a long time, it was a Black Christian oasis in a segregated desert.

When Martin, Jr., completed his religious education in Boston, he came back to Atlanta and became assistant to his father as pastor of Ebenezer.

By nature and by training, both King, Sr., and I always firmly stood by what we thought was right. There was no backing down and no compromise, friendship not-withstanding. Once, my friendship with King, Sr., hit a temporary snag.

It was the premiere of the picture based on Margaret Mitchell's novel, *Gone With the Wind*, in Atlanta. Though still young, I was elected President of the Atlanta Chapter of the NAACP. It was just before my installation as president at the Wheat Street Baptist Church that Reverend King's church choir and the choir of Bethel A.M.E. (a church once presided over by Bishop Henry McNeil Turner, one of the most outspoken defenders of Blacks) had dressed in antebellum or slave costumes to sing in front of both the movie theater and at the Grand Ball City Auditorium, neither of which Blacks could enter. I had strong commitments regarding discrimination and segregation, and I had worked for equalization of teacher salaries and the eradication of discrimination in other areas as part of my platform as President of the NAACP.

In my speech of acceptance of the presidency, I did not favor the churches' participation in the programs connected with *Gone With the Wind* and condemned their action as being "offensive to Blacks and stinking to high heaven." One minister walked out of the church. The next day, Reverend King came into the bank where I had my small office, and from the lobby stated his opinion of me and my actions.

He forecasted a rather doubtful future for me in business if I ever dared to attack the churches in Atlanta. He said he would see to it that I got none of their insurance. I assured him I could never be bought, even if it cost me my business.

He stormed out and I went on with my work. As a result of our natures and our firm commitments to stand behind what we believed, eventually we got to respect each other more. One thing we did agree upon was that we both could be depended upon to say what we meant and to mean what we said.

Martin Luther King, Sr., and I saw each other's kids grow up. We saw Atlanta under Mayor Hartsfield's administration grow "too busy to hate." When Reverend Vernon Johns, who was pastor of Dexter Avenue Church resigned, he was the "John the Baptist" who opened the door through which Martin, Jr., was destined to go.

I had learned to enjoy the sermons of Martin, Jr., and knew of his deep religious commitment. When I learned Dexter needed a minister, I thought the young King was the type to fill the void. It had always been a difficult church to pastor because of the nature of its membership, professional and college-oriented, and well entrenched leadership. Reverend Johns was from West Virginia and was considered one of the nation's most brilliant preachers, even if unorthodoxed.

I contacted my parents, and through them and my friend, Bob Nesbitt, Martin, Jr., was extended an invitation for a trial sermon. He was later accepted as minister to the church. I was asked to "charge" the church at his installation service.

I knew Dexter Avenue Baptist Church and I knew Martin, Jr. Montgomery was primed for the young dynamic leader. She had too long lived up to the Indian name of "Alabama" for which the state was named, meaning "Here we rest." Few changes had taken place, progress was slow, and no one dared challenge the status quo. A few families dominated the economic and political life of the city, and Blacks accepted, of necessity, second-class citizenship and there was no central leadership that was effective. Paternalism and favoritism were the general practices, and a few Blacks were anointed by Whites to maintain the customs and traditions of the Old South which were segregation and complete separation or suffer grave consequences.

In my "charge" to the church, I wanted to make a breathtaking speech in the church of my childhood and in the presence of my parents and friends. Yet, being a Sunday School teacher for so long in my adopted church, I wanted to be biblical in my charge as well. When I stepped up to the pulpit, I leaned over the podium to dramatize what I wanted to say:

"Before Martin Luther King, Jr., leaves Montgomery, he will put a plumb line on this city and shake the Cradle of the Confederacy from Center to circumference."

There was applause.

I did not know, nor did I have any idea I was being prophetic. Only the future was to prove how right I "accidentally" predicted Martin's future. At this time, there was no bus boycott, no great racial issue even on the horizon or in the minds of anyone in Montgomery. Martin preached at Dexter, and Ralph D. Abernathy sermonized at First Baptist Church, formally pastored by another fearless leader, Reverend A.J. Stokes before and during World War I. (Stokes, during a race riot in 1920, challenged the Ku Klux Klan to come and get him. He said he would be waiting for them! Both he and his son, Hugo, who had returned as an officer in the Army stood their ground unmolested.)

Martin, Jr., had the great gift of speech and the ability to hold an audience spellbound, with both his logic and wisdom. When the Black citizens for the first time rose up in righteous indignation, they sought a leader whom they could trust and one whom they felt the people would follow. Even though Martin, Jr., tried to avoid accepting the position of leader, mainly because he felt someone who had been there longer should be chosen, the people insisted he should be the one.

When Mrs. Rosa Parks, whose husband was a barber at Atlas

Barber Shop, where my father used to have an office in his construction business, refused to give up her seat in the section of the bus designated for Whites, she was arrested for violating the law of segregation. Blacks began to seek out additional leadership to challenge the system. This was the beginning of the bus boycott and the birth of the modern Civil Rights Movement that not only shook the Cradle of the Confederacy, but of the country and the world.

For the boycott to be effective, and because Blacks lived, as in most southern cities, some distance from their place of employment, some form of alternative transportation had to be provided. Car pools were organized by all the Black churches; however, there was a limit to both cars and drivers available. Central dispatch stations were set up and schedules and routes were set up to parallel the bus lines.

When the word got out, the nation was awakened to what was taking place in Montgomery. For probably the first time, Christian churches all over the country joined in the effort to make the boycott a success. Many Whites and other religious groups of goodwill gave their support. Transportation in the form of cars and station wagons of all makes and models began pouring into Montgomery. They were distributed to some 19 churches. In spite of the tremendous help, all was not smooth sailing and White opposition was created by some of the highest levels of society.

The boycott was 100 percent successful until the insurance companies cancelled the insurance on all vehicles used in the bus boycott, under pressure from the segregationists. It was against the law to drive a public carrier without public liability and property damage insurance. Not having vehicles brought the boycott abruptly to a halt.

At this time, I was past vice-president of the fire and casualty insurance company which I had helped found. We could write insurance covering only physical damage. No auto liability and property damage could be written by us.

We found ourselves in the untenable position of having to depend on an unfriendly and antagonistic source of supply for a basic need - auto insurance. No Black insurance company in existence was capable of coming to King's rescue.

Martin, Jr., called me and told me his problem. I had excellent contacts for placing insurance through my agency for those risks which our company was not qualified to accept. I was sure, at first, I would have no problem, and called one of my sources which had a substantial volume of my business. I told them I needed insurance on 19 station wagons operated by 19 churches in Montgomery, involved in the bus boycott.

The reply was, "T.M., you know how we feel about you and we appreciate all the business you have with us. Our firm would do anything we could to help you personally, but the word had been passed throughout the South that no company should touch this situation in Montgomery. We appreciate your concern and we are sympathetic with what is taking place. Since you have a young business and are highly regarded by the insurance industry, I would advise you to stay away from trying to place this insurance or you may be forced out of business."

I became indignant and expressed surprise at the position they too were taking, but I also realized that they would have difficulty and could have their own businesses jeopardized if they came to King's rescue. I also knew what my position had to be, notwithstanding my dependence on the insurance industry for both my own business and the recently organized insurance company my friends and I had founded with agencies in Alabama and Georgia. I had no idea where to turn, but I knew I had an obligation to King. I had some responsibility for his being in Montgomery as pastor of Dexter Avenue Baptist Church.

An hour after I hung up the phone, a member of the firm with whom I had worked closely called me back. "T.M," he said, "I have been thinking how I could help you. I know a man in Chicago who represents Lloyd's, London. He doesn't even look South. I will call him and give him your name and our relationship, and then you call him, maybe he can help you."

I thanked him and had decided to place all on the altar for what I considered a righteous cause, even if it would cost me my business and my future. There was a principle involved which I could not compromise.

I made the call to Chicago. The man I talked to was most considerate and expressed his personal views on the justification of what was happening in Montgomery. He said he would do all he could to help me get the station wagons insured, but not the physical damage, only the liability and property insurance.

He asked me the names of the 19 churches. I didn't know the names of all churches. Then he asked for the make, models, and other information on each station wagon. I didn't have that information either. He asked, "What do you have?"

I replied that 19 churches in Montgomery had one station wagon each and I would have to get the details and send them to him as soon as King and Abernathy could get the information to me. I asked if he could, in the meantime, get a temporary binder, pending the receipt of details.

He asked if they were all Christian churches. I don't know why he asked that question, but my answer was, "Yes, they are." I was right, but I didn't know it then.

He said, "I'll be back in touch shortly after I cable London." Within 24 hours, he called and said, "I have been authorized by Lloyd's to issue a binder which will read, '19 station wagons owned by 19 churches, Montgomery, Alabama.' Hurry and send the details so that the policy can be issued, but this binder will get the station wagons rolling again, and I'm mailing it air mail special to you. Good luck. The premium will be approximately $3,000."

In all communications please quote the following reference	
5 3 6	C 71211

FORM J (A)

LLOYD'S, LONDON.

Assured   CHRISTIAN CHURCHES.

Premium   U.S.$3,040.00

Policy and Stamp

Date of Expiry   17th September, 1957.

The Assured is requested to read this Policy, and, if incorrect, return it immediately for alteration

In the event of any occurrence likely to result in a claim under this Policy, immediate notice should be given to :—

ALEXANDER & CO.
▷INSURANCE OF ALL KINDS◁
208 AUBURN AVE. N. E., ATLANTA, GA. 30303
PHONE 521-0549

Lloyd's, London policy issued to Alexander & Company which insured automobiles used in the Montgomery Bus Boycott.

LLOYD'S POLICY

(Subscribed only by Underwriting Members of Lloyd's all of whom have complied with the requirements of the Assurance Companies Acts 1909 and 1946 as to security and otherwise.)

Form approved by Lloyd's
Underwriters' Fire and
Non-Marine Association.

Any person not an Underwriting Member of Lloyd's subscribing this Policy, or any person uttering the same if so subscribed, will be liable to be proceeded against under Lloyd's Acts.

100%
Printed at Lloyd's, London, England.
JJ-14

Whereas   CHRISTIAN CHURCHES.

of   Montgomery, Alabama.

(hereinafter called " the Assured "),   have   paid   U.S.$3,040.00

Premium or Consideration to Us, who have hereunto subscribed our Names to

Insure against Loss as follows :—   BODILY INJURY & PROPERTY DAMAGE INSURANCE.

To Indemnify the Assured as more fully set forth in the wording attached hereto,

which is hereby declared to be incorporated in and to form a part of this Policy.

No. C | 71211

during the period commencing with the   Eighteenth   day of   September, 1956
and ending with the   Seventeenth   of   September, 1957, both days inclusive.

If the Assured shall make any claim knowing the same to be false or fraudulent, as regards amount or otherwise, this Policy shall become void, and all claim thereunder shall be forfeited.

NOW KNOW YE, that We the Underwriters, members of the Syndicate(s) whose definitive Number(s) in the Schedule hereto are set out in the Table overleaf, or attached overleaf, hereby bind Ourselves, each for his own part and not one for Another, our Heirs, Executors, and Administrators, and in respect of his due proportion only, to pay or make good to the Assured or the Assured's Executors, Administrators, and Assigns, or to indemnify him or them against all such Loss, Damage or Liability as aforesaid (subject to the conditions herein expressed) not exceeding the Sum of   limits of liability as stated herein.

Lloyd's, London policy showing premium amount and specified coverage.

SCHEDULE.

Name & Address of Assured.	Description of Automobile With Serial &/or Motor No
1. Mt. Gillead Baptist Church 1402 Vine St., Montgomery, Alabama.	1956 Chevrolet Station Wagon Serial No. 0313314F562.
2. Oak Street A.M.E. Zion Church 2764 West Edgemont Ave., Montgomery, Ala.	1956 Chevrolet Station Wagon Morot No. 0323304F56Y
3. Mt. Zion A.M.E. Zion Church 657 South Holt St., Montgomery, Alabama.	1956 Ford Country Sedan Motor No. M6UX-178278
4. Hall Street Baptish Church 700 South Hall St., Montgomery, Alabama.	1956 Chevrolet Station Wagon Motor No. 958295F56G
5. Beulah Baptist Church 623 Unkon St., Montgomery,. Alabama.	1956 Chevrolet Station Wagon Motor No. 0282672F56F
6. Old Ship A.M.E. Zion Church 477 Holcomb St., Montgomery	1956 Chevrolet Station Wagon Motor No. 0282672F56F
7. Maggie Street Baptist Church 642 Maggie St., Montgomery, Alabama	1956 Chevrolet Station Wagon Motor No. 02420404T56Z
8. Bethel Baptist Church 1112 Mobile Road, Montgomery, Alabama	1956 Chevrolet Station Wagon Motor No. 029103F56Z
9. Bell Street Baptist Church Oak & N. Robinson St., Montgomery, Ala.	1956 Chevrolet Station Wagon Motor No. 056F144193
10. Dexter Avenue Baptist Church 454 Dexter Ave., Montgomery, Alabama	1956 Chevrolet Station Wagon Motor No. 0382309F56F
11. Shiloah Baptist Church 801 Felham St., Montgomery, Alabama	1956 Ford Station Wagon Motor No. M6UX159665
12. Bryant Street Baptist Church 729 Adeline St., Montgomery, Alabama	1956 Ford Station Wagon Motor No. M6D4150820
13. Holt Street Baptist Church 847 W. Jefferson Davis Ave., Montgomery, Ala.	1956 Chevrolet Station Wagon Motor No. 0389451F56F
14. St. John A.M.E. Church 809 Madison Ave., Montgomery, Alabama	1956 Chevrolet Station Wagon Motor No. 0164351I560
15. Hutchinson Street Baptist Church 924 Hutchinson St., Montgomery, Alabama	1956 Chevrolet Station Wagon Motor No. 0069986T56F
16. First Baptish Church 347 No. Ripley St., Montgomery, Alabama	1956 Chevrolet Station Wagon Motor No. 0274351F56F
17. First C.M.E. Church 716 Glass St., Montgomery, Alabama	1956 Chevrolet Station Wagon Motor No. 0296785F56F
18. Lilly Baptist Church 2141 Winifred St., Montomery, Alabama	1956 Chevrolet Station Wagon No. 0427883-F 562
19. Cannan Hill Baptist Church Thornington Rd., Montgomery, Alabama	1951 Ford Station Wagon No. B1BA-165307.

Names of churches and descriptions of automobiles insured by Lloyd's,
London, with Alexander &Company.

I delivered it to Montgomery and that solved their insurance problems because I had decided to take the physical damage in my own company. I was afraid to clear it with the Board of Directors and never did. A series of bad accidents could have wrecked the company and me.

But God was with us and there was only one small loss of less than $200 during the entire year. Lloyd's, London did not have a single loss. The drivers were careful and, under the most difficult situation of driving defensively against aggravations of those opposing the boycott, developed an almost perfect record.

I eventually got the details on each station wagon and in about 60 days the actual policy was delivered. I kept the original master policy from Lloyd's with the names of all of the churches and the station wagon owned by each, dated September 1956, but issued in November 1956, in my possession in a safety deposit box.

At the end of the year, the Montgomery Improvement Association gave a banquet for the bus drivers, held at the Ben Moore Hotel, a Black-owned hotel on High Jackson Street in Montgomery. I was asked to come down to Montgomery as the guest speaker. While giving my speech in the banquet hall on the top floor, something resembling acid was poured on some of the cars parked on the street. I noted that some attitudes would take a long time to change.

This, however, was not the last time I dealt closely with Martin Luther King, Jr. His life was in constant danger and subject to threats. On one occasion, while he was out of the city, some of Martin's followers had been jailed in Montgomery. He decided to make the perilous trip back as soon as he could.

On his was back to Montgomery, he stopped in Atlanta to be with his parents. His father asked him to remain over and talk to some of his close friends. His mother and father were trying to persuade him not to return to Montgomery. Among the ones asked to meet at their home were A.T. Walden, C.R. Yates, C.A. Scott, Bishop Sherman

Green, Dr. Benjamin Mays, Dr. Rufus Clement, and myself. Mrs. Coretta Scott King and King's mother joined us.

King, Sr., explained he was trying to get his son not to go back to Montgomery and turn himself over to the police. He was afraid Martin's mother would have a heart attack and the strain on the family was more than they could take.

After listening to us, Martin, Jr., made his statement of appreciation for our concerns, but said, "I have reached the point of no return. It would be the height of cowardice for me to stay away. I must go back. I'd rather be in jail for ten years than desert my people now, while my friends and associates are being arrested."

His father broke into tears and said, "If this is my son's decision, I am going back with him."

We knew he was right and we had to support his position, and hope and pray for his safety.

I returned to Dexter on December 13, 1957, to be the banquet speaker celebrating the 80th anniversary of my church. The speech, *"The Role of the Controversial Church,"* was apropos for what was happening. After giving some of the history of the church, I said:

"When in His good time He was ready to make this spot the cornerstone of a new temple for racial justice and human dignity, when He wanted a voice that could speak fearlessly and keep his head, demand respect, remain humble, who had simple honesty, deep and unswerving devotion to his own people, and could love his enemies until they recanted, conscious-stricken, before the impact of his disarming and dynamic personality. He got a young man who could walk with crowds and keep his virtue, walk with kings and not lose the common touch. It may have taken eighty years to get the job ready for the man, but only twenty-eight years to get the man ready for the job. No leader in the history of this church or any church had done so much in so short a time against so many odds to restore dignity and self-respect to the darker peoples of the world as Martin Luther King, Jr.

"Dexter is poised on the threshold of its destiny; the purpose for which God conditioned us is now upon us. I charge you on your eightieth birthday to be worthy of the challenge and the responsibilities for which you were chosen and carefully prepared to assume.

"I'm told that when a pilot flies a plane without aid of instruments, clouds can be very dangerous. But between them there are the corridors, the shafts of light, the open spaces. If you are piloting a plane and are flying visually and find yourself in a cloud, you search for these corridors, if around you are clouds. But along the corridors straight ahead is visibility, your path to safety.

"We have found our corridor in the clouds, a shaft of light, a clear path to freedom, to wisdom, to all good.

"There, too, is the all-important 'Man in the tower' who keeps in touch with us. We have to heed His voice. We have to realize, too, that when we go to a certain distance, we get out of the range of the Voice that got us on our course and the inner voice from another tower gives us guidance. We have to know when it's time to tune in on the tower ahead and get out of the one behind.

"Our real job has just begun. Let's not become weary or satisfied or overwhelmed by what we have already accomplished. This is a day like no other day, and much will be required of us. Nothing short of fulfilling the maximum obligation of a Christian church will be acceptable, and that is not possible until every man has come alive inside to the decency, equality, and dignity of every other man.

'Wherewith shall I come before the Lord, and bow myself before the most high God. Shall I come with burnt offerings, or calves of one year old?
'Will the Lord be satisfied with thousands of rams, or ten thousand rivers of oil? Shall I give my first-born for my transgressions, or the fruit of my body, for the sins of my soul?
'Thou hast been shown, O man, what is good, and what doth the Lord require of thee, but that thou do justly, love mercy, and walk humbly with thy God. "

When the bus situation was finally settled in Montgomery, and Martin, Jr., had emerged as the undisputed leader in the Civil Rights Movement, he resigned the pastorage of Dexter and decided to make Atlanta his home base. The Southern Christian Leadership Conference Movement (SCLC) was beginning. However, the movement still had many enemies.

Concerns existed about the likelihood of SCLC funds in Montgomery banks being attacked for some reason. I, with my friends and former teacher, L.D. Milton, President of Citizens Trust Bank, had Martin Luther, Jr., and Ralph Abernathy meet at the Hunter Street Branch of the YMCA and arranged the transfer of funds in Montgomery to the Atlanta Black-owned Citizens Trust Company.

In Atlanta, I gave SCLC temporary office space in my building until they could arrange for more adequate office space. Eventually, the SCLC was headquartered in the Masonic Building.

Fire bombings were not unheard of during this period and all of us were concerned about the safety of our meeting places. Once, Martin, Jr., wanted a safe place to have a press conference where he would make one of his announcements relating to the Civil Rights Movement. I arranged for him to have the executive Suite of University Plaza Apartments, which my family owned in the center of the Atlanta University complex on Fair Street.

I worked with King and the movement wherever I could, both on the front lines and in the background along with many other dedicated civic leaders and businessmen, loudly protesting injustice or quietly oiling the wheels of the Civil Rights machinery.

Sadly, one day, the evils of the world caught up with Martin Luther King, Jr. On the day of his assassination, Reverend Sam Williams and I, along with members of the Community Relations Committee, were having a meeting at the Jewish temple on Peachtree Street, headed by Rabbi Rothchild. The telephone rang and Reverend Sam Williams, head of the Community Relations Committee and pastor of Friendship Church, went to answer the call.

He came back and announced that Martin had been shot in Memphis, Tennessee. He turned the meeting over to me and left, saying he would report back to us. It was later when he called and said Martin had been killed. We all broke down in tears and abruptly adjourned the meeting. We were hurt to our souls and made numb by the news. It was like our world had come to a sudden end.

We rushed to our homes, and all night hung on the radio and television. His speeches were being replayed, messages from around the world came in, sadness engulfed the air, restraint gave way to violence and all hell broke loose all over the country. Words such as these were frequently spoken: Out of the debris and wrongs of the times, a new world is still being born, and it is through his life and death we know - We Shall Overcome Someday - and the dream he had will never die.

In the course of the Civil Rights Movement before King's death, nothing was changed overnight. While I saw myself as a banner man, I did my share of picketing with the time I could spare. In 1961, I was active in picketing the Rich Department Store which discriminated against Blacks. I wore a sign which read, "Wear old clothes with new dignity. Don't Buy Here!" My wife was involved more deeply in this campaign. She cancelled her account and this fact deeply upset the ownership of Rich's Department Store.

In the end, none of our sacrifices compared with those risked and then taken by Dr. Martin Luther King, Jr.

Progress Through Coalition Building

Your deeds today will build the walkway to the house you will live in tomorrow.

T.M. Alexander, Sr.

While Martin Luther King, Jr.'s tactics of direct, nonviolent protest were effective and a necessary part of breaking down the walls of segregation, there still remained "nuts and bolts" work across a broad panorama which was done under the auspices of W.L. Calloway's Action Forum. Calloway, a good friend, was responsible for creating this body in 1971. His efforts paralleled my undertaking on the political front when I ran for Alderman in 1957, and State Senate in 1961.

Even though there existed a sort of loose relationship between the Black and White leadership, it was on a one-to-one personal basis. When there was a potential problem or concern, someone would call someone else of influence to assist in a solution. Gradually, a few Blacks were placed on the Better Housing Commission, Community Relations Commission, and the Atlanta's Ethnic Committee. These were more or less political considerations for Black supporters whose votes were beginning to mean something.

The power base was not centered entirely in the political arena. To a degree, it was also subject to the economic arena, and the business leadership of the city. Together, these were the support basis and the key to progress on all fronts in Atlanta. This fact had been the genius of Atlanta's uniqueness among southern cities.

The one thing lacking was a more formal organization of Black and White leadership that met regularly and with mutual respect and dedication to Atlanta's progress in every conceivable area. The whole idea and concept originated with W.L. "Bill" Calloway.

Calloway went to see Mills B. Lane to explain his idea. Mills Lane, in 1971, was one of Atlanta's leading bankers as president and chief executive officer of the Citizens and Southern National Bank. He was known as one of the most innovative and unusual bankers of his day. Although well known as a banker, he was also a political influence. Lane represented openly the power structure of the city as a spokesman who dared take an uncharted position just to see if an idea could flourish.

In a letter dated September 29, 1971, after having met with Calloway, Mills wrote, "Dear Bill, I enjoyed our conversation this morning tremendously! It was most stimulating, and I can't tell you how great it is that your group took the initiative to develop a plan to bring us all together."

Calloway had wisely selected eight, primarily young up-and-coming Black business leaders, thereby giving the future leadership among Blacks an introduction to corresponding White leaders. It could not have been successful if Bill had not been smart enough to realize that a new leadership was being created, with a different style.

It was interesting to see the similarity of thinking between Mills B. Lane and Bill Calloway in their prospective lists of persons to form the initial committee. There were about two of the "old guard" leaders on each list, just enough to give sober and wise counsel, and most of all, the "green light" and blessings of the power structure.

After suggesting in his letter to Calloway to appoint eight members each, Mills Lane added, "This will give us a good mixture of young businessmen in town, older businessmen, and important people who have the future of Atlanta in their hearts."

This was the catalyst that created a new resurgence in Atlanta and a Black-and-White coalition to address all community affairs. The original committee was composed of those eight Whites and eight Blacks in business, civic, and political affairs in the community. The following persons were the original members of the Atlanta Liaison Committee:

Black Members

Mr. John Cox, Executive Director
    Butler Street Young Men's Christian Association
Mr. Jesse Hill, Jr., Vice President
    Atlanta Life Insurance Company
Mr. Lonnie King, President
    Atlanta Branch of the NAACP
Mr. Lyndon Wade, Executive Director
    Atlanta Urban League
Mr. Fletcher Coombs, Executive Vice-President
    Mutual Federal Saving and Loan Association
Mr. Herman J. Russell, President
    H.J. Russell Plastering Company
Mr. Charles Reynolds, President
    Citizens Trust Company
Alderman Q.V. Williamson, President
    Williamson Reality Company
Mr. James Paschal, President
    Paschal Brothers Motor Hotel and Restaurant
Mr. W.L. Calloway, President
    Calloway Realty Company

White Members
Mr. Tom Cousins, President
        Cousins Properties Incorporated
Attorney Mike Trotter
        Member of the firm of Alsten, Miller and Gaines
Mr. Tom Beebe, President
        Delta Airlines
Mr. Billy Sterne, President
        Trust Company of Georgia
Mr. John Portman, President
        Peachtree Center
Mr. Lee Burge, President
        Retail Credit Corporation
Mr. Paul Austin, President
        Coco-Cola Company
Mr. L. Gellerstedt, President-elect
        Atlanta Chamber of Commerce
Mr. Mills B. Lane, President
        Citizens and Southern National Bank

The committee members met separately first and were briefed on the overall objective of the coalition and its interest in addressing current community problems. At a joint meeting, an agenda of priorities was presented, as follows:
1. Economic Development - Jobs
2. Education
3. Housing
4. Consolidation, Annexation, Charter Division, Cooperation of County and Municipal Governments
5. Political Leadership

6. Civic Leadership
7. Zoning and Planning

In the initial meeting of the group, Calloway made these remarks: "First, before I begin, if any genuine results are to accrue from my observations today, I think it will require that you try to adjust your mental attitude regarding what I might say; not with the customary feeling of the need to rebut it, but, rather to try to be analytically receptive in order that some new innovative approaches to our common problems might possibly ensue.

"Second, I ask that you sympathize with me in my predicament standing up here. I am no authority or 'Mister-Know-It-All.' I'm no big shot showing off and I'm no leader bringing you 'the word.' I'm just another citizen of Atlanta, like you, concerned about a town I was born in and love deeply.

"All of you are equally aware of what is happening to big cities all over America; of their rapid deterioration, both physically as well as spiritually and morally. Does this just have to happen to Atlanta? Do we just sit around until it does? Or do we show the nation, in this instance, as we have demonstrated in so many others, that we possess the intestinal fortitude and leadership to cope with this 'new happening,' instead of just being another 'Me, too'?

"Atlanta is already beginning to experience a few of the symptoms of decay. And there are people here who have been quietly, and unfortunately in many instances, behind closed doors discussing the situation. A lot of the discussion, and here again I say unfortunately, has been carried on with the same old customary racial overtones.

"So, let's open the blinds, raise the shades, put all 52 of the cards on the table and, as the saying goes, 'come clean this once' as we ponder these questions. Is there anyone here today who honestly believes that our city's problems can be solved separately? Does anybody here feel we can ever truly escape from each other (even those who have already made reservations on the moon)?

"Finally, are we ready? And this was the last question I posed to Mills the other day. I mean, are we without any hypocrisy, truly ready as men, not Black and not White, but as men created by God to live on His earth, if not as brothers, at least as fellowmen?

"If so, then 'look out' other cities. If you think Atlanta has set the pace in the South in the past years, watch it set the pace for America and the world in the future."

From there, the meeting discussed the White flight from the city, the deterioration of downtown, the responsibilities of newly increased Black political leadership. Martin Luther King, Jr., and the Civil Rights Movement may have won the war, but maintaining an economic viability and civil atmosphere was the problem the Action Forum saw before it, not too different from the same kind of battle I was fighting after 1931.

The Action Forum proved to be a success. I had a measure of good fortune in business that in conjunction with the Forum, was part of the Atlanta *Story of the Century* from which I hoped those who came after us would gain much profit.

Each generation should build upon the legacies of the past, but each generation must first leave a legacy that future generations can build upon.

The Legacy of Fellowship

Remember those who cleared the path and built the bridges you crossed.

T.M. Alexander, Sr.

The greatest joy that came from years of sustained success in such a highly competitive field as the insurance business was the numerous relationships I established. Some lasted a few days, weeks, months, or years. Some continued even longer than my formal entrance into business. Having abiding relationships with persons of worth was a drive within the inner core of myself.

The strongest relationships became friendships, and the best of these, in turn, developed into fellowships. There was a distinction between friendship and fellowship, even though there can be no real and meaningful fellowship without friendship. One may have known and liked other persons and had friendly feelings or behavior toward them, and yet never created a real fellowship.

When a friendship developed into feelings of brotherhood and sharing, a companionship was created which went beyond the limitations of being a friend. A kinship was developed that became a fellowship. Each person in the fellowship shared the dreams, aspirations, and desires of the other. Likewise, they shared and anguished over the failures, misfortunes, and unrealized dreams of their companions. Not only did they share in the good or bad fortunes, they even offered, at a great sacrifice, tangible support to help in overcoming whatever misfortune existed.

A real fellowship had great power and influence in overcoming the trials and difficulties in one's life, because you knew that whatever happened there would be a demonstration of fellowship that came forth in your time of need. However, it was a two-way street in that you received the by-product or the reward of having demonstrated the spirit of fellowship in your own life. It wasn't something you work at with the idea of reaping the reward. It emanated from your natural behavior and attitude toward people and life itself.

You may go through life with many friends whom you see and associate with frequently. You may like each other and have a common interest in business, socially or otherwise, and yet a fellowship does not evolve. Fellowship was only limited by capability, not desire or concern.

I had been fortunate in experiencing and creating many fellowships. It had become a habit of my life and I believed in the intangible power of fellowship.

My oldest living friend and I enjoyed a fellowship approaching 60 years. We had shared our fortunes and misfortunes, our triumphs and failures, with equal concern and support. We knew all about each other's weaknesses and strengths. We differed at times, but hung together against any attempt to disrupt our fellowship. We do not need to affirm that we could depend on each other if a crisis occurred in our life or any members of our family, or anyone committed to our fellowship. Our relationship didn't require the approval or sanction of anyone outside ourselves. We respected the right to differ when we see a situation from a different perspective. We may go in two different directions to reach the same objective, but no matter who got there first, we were side-by-side in the end.

William "Bill" Calloway and I had been together since we were twelve and fourteen years old respectively. We played together and we faced opponents together. We started earning money as kids with the making and selling of home-made pocketbooks from automobile inner tubes split open in reverse. While there was an interlude of separation while we attended different colleges, we managed to get together from time to time in the summers.

After our college days, Calloway became a teacher in the Atlanta school system. Calloway continued to teach but he worked with me part-time. We built a growing business and I knew he would be able to make more in real estate, so I offered him $25.00 more a month than the $75.00 he was paid teaching. That was the beginning of our partnership in Alexander-Calloway Realty Co., and the Alexander and Company Agency. We both saw a half century going great.

The next great lasting friendship almost immediately developing into a fellowship came in the fall of 1925. It was my second year in the Academy at Morehouse when "Little Richard from Rome (Georgia)" enlivened the campus with his vibrant personality. Richard Carlton Hackney was chubby and round-faced with a bubbly personality. He would knock on the door of any room in the dormitory and announce, "It's Little Richard from Rome," usually selling apples or something else to pick up a few nickels to spend at the corner for hot dogs.

Our friendship was immediate. We went through high school and college together. We used to say, "We came to college to make friends and influence people." We cut some afternoon classes to take in the theater, which led to us staying in summer school in 1927 to catch up. We arranged to go to the tobacco farm in summer school to work. We settled down in our freshman year to serious business and we became roommates.

His ambition was to become a doctor; mine to enter the field of business. We both became debaters and graduated with honors. He went to Meharry Medical College in Nashville, and I went for some practical training and employment with North Carolina Mutual Life Insurance Company in Durham, North Carolina.

I kept in constant touch with my friend, offering to give him any help I could. When he needed a stethoscope, I sent him one. He said it was his first. My wife and I were at his graduation and insisted that he march with his class. He was not able to afford the cap and gown, but we got one and my wife made the green tassel to replace theBlack one on the cap. We were the only ones close to him to witness the graduation. We drove our second-hand car and rented a room in a private home. At the time my wife was pregnant with our second daughter.

He did a long term internship at Homer G. Phillip Hospital in St. Louis, and we remained in constant contact. He was without a father and his entire support came from his mother and summer employment throughout his college career. I was a little more fortunate and we shared, as brothers, whatever we had, and we worked odd jobs while in school.

By the time he had completed his internship, two of Atlanta's leading surgeons had died. Knowing his specialty was surgery, I urged him to consider practicing in Atlanta. I immediately tied up one of the deceased surgeon's office space pending his acceptance.

When he did come to Atlanta, I automatically became his one-man P.R. team. I knew he could not advertise his expertise or capabilities as a surgeon, but hearing how efficient he was, I started a word-of-mouth campaign like this: "I understand we will have a new surgeon coming to town, with eyes in the end of his fingers. They say he can operate from either side of the table, and take a left-hand appendix from the right side."

I admit I did not know whether all of this made sense, but it sounded good and the word spread. Professionally, he actually lived up to my exaggerated publicity.

We both were making some progress, but his was more immediate because his skills as a surgeon were in great demand. There was a shortage of Black surgeons in Atlanta. We made some joint investments and made some extra money. By this time, I had an active real estate company headed by Calloway.

With the cash I had and the construction loan from the bank, I was able to buy a small lot next to Citizens Trust Bank on Auburn Avenue to build a one-story structure to house my insurance agency and real estate firm.

When Richard heard what I was planning to do, he said the land was too valuable not to go to a second story. At that time, I told him I would need $3,000 more in cash. This was a test of our long fellowship. I had stood for his office furniture a few years before when he began practice. He lived next to my house, and we shared food before he married.

When he married, I had already built a new home in 1941, and he and his bride lived with me and my family as one family. He grabbed at the opportunity to do something for me, and, to my utter surprise one morning, he walked into my office, smiling as usual, and said, "Rooms, hold out your hands," and without entering the office, pitched to me, as he counted, "one, two, three thousand dollars," $1,000 cash in each stack.

Saying, as he turned to leave, "Put that second story on and when you get it refinanced, bring that back the same way so that I can put it back where I had it." Smiling, he left. This experience, I will never forget. We spent the remainder of his life sharing our experiences, our families, and all the joys of a genuine fellowship. It left a void in my life when he passed. On his deathbed, he told me to keep in touch with his family and especially his four sons. This charge I held as a sacred trust. He would be proud of their achievements in their respective fields. I knew of no more perfect a performance as a legacy of their father and the opportunity to enjoy a continuing fellowship.

I had other fellowships, even with Whites, such as John Sibley and John Charles Whitner. My pleasant relationship with Mr. Whitner was a tremendous asset to me. I could not have achieved my success without his help that formed the basis for many other ventures into the hitherto untried and untested areas of bi-racial cooperation. It had not only been a pattern for me in business, but in many community problems where understanding and friendly cooperation were indispensable ingredients.

In the beginning of my career, I never realized that I would become involved in numerous activities and situations in the years ahead where I could still draw strength and hope from this fellowship. It would always remain a source of inspiration and hope when the way seemed dark.

I couldn't help but remember the April day in 1960 when my friend, John Charles Whitner died. It was interspersed with sunshine and showers, dreary one moment and glowingly bright the next day. The dogwood blossoms and azaleas were radiant even against the cloudy skies, as though they had captured sprinklings of sunlight as an interlude of the darkened moments.

I had taught my regular Sunday School class, even though my heart was heavy as I contemplated the reality I would soon face upon leaving church to pay my respects to the family of my dearest friend. He had passed on the night before.

I drove my car through the city traffic, out over the winding and rolling hills of suburban Atlanta and, at times, I was uncertain whether it was the rain on the windshield or the tears in my eyes that made seeing difficult. Even though I had expected this great soul and fine Christian gentleman to soon be called to his reward, the emptiness was there, and I could feel deep inside the void that was left. I thought back over the many years of friendship and business relationships we had experienced, including, the many mutual friends such as Mr. Oberdorfer who worked closely with Whitner and me.

I tried to think of any occasion or any circumstance in which either of us had a single disagreement, even though we had handled jointly, or for each other, many substantial transactions. Come to think of it, we never had a written contract between us, except once, and that was to insure the perpetuation of our business relationship against those who sought to break it.

Our friendship transcended the narrow confines of race and the crippling influences of prejudice. We met on a lofty plateau of mutual respect and goodwill. Our handshake was a signed contract, legally sealed by mutual trust.

When I entered his living room, filled with his family and friends, they all knew who I was because he had shared our experiences with everyone he knew. We were not ashamed or afraid for those who knew us to know our mutual respect and high regard for each other.

His beloved widow and I placed our arms around each other's shoulders and we wept over our mutual loss. I shared with those present some of the experiences we had during his lifetime, the amusing ones, and the more serious ones. He had often said, "If anything happens to me, go to my family, and see that they are properly protected and advised."

I had kept my contracts in life with him. I vowed to keep them in death. I left his home and was told I was expected to be with the family at the funeral. I went by the mortuary to see him for the last time. I stayed in the room for a while and looked at his lifeless body peacefully asleep. I could not resist the urge to touch his hand, and there was a warmth through the coldness. I had never touched a lifeless human being before.

The next day I would follow him to his final resting place. Because of his kindness to me, a whole new area of opportunity had opened to Blacks in the South and his memorial shall be forever.

It was he who gave me faith and courage to face the future, even with the odds against me. I shall never forget his words, "Do a good job and they will look for you instead of you looking for them. Someday you'll have your own companies, owned and operated by your own people. What you are doing in fire insurance, you'll eventually do in all lines of insurance."

One week before he passed, I had the opportunity to tell him, "We have been approved as a Multiple Line Insurance Company, the first in America among Negroes."

"I am happy for you. Remember, I told you so," he responded.

And, as though he was just waiting to see his prophecy fulfilled, he folded his arms and departed. But his memory continue to strengthen my faith in the innate morality of the South, and its eventual emergence to its maximum potential. He helped his prophecy come true, and passed on to his reward.

That was remembering him at the end of our friendship. The day he agreed to help, however, was just as memorable.

In 1989, Mr. Whitney's daughter, Victoria, came to the opening of my new office in downtown Atlanta. She brought with her a paperweight in the shape of a pile of gold coins. Inscribed on it was, "Your friendship has been golden to me." This was a gift that I had given to Mr. Whitner many years ago. She gave it back to me as a token of the long friendship I had with her father.

A City Adopted by a Corporation

*Never go to the banquet table with nothing but an appetite.
You may end up with crumbs.*

T.M. Alexander, Sr.

Most corporations are best known for their products and\or services. All corporations strive for higher profits for its stockholders and better salaries for its employees. But corporate interest beyond higher profits and customer recognition vary depending on corporate philosophy, founders, and the degree of dedication to causes above corporate interest.

Sometimes the birth place of a corporation, like the birth place of an individual, may or may not afford the greatest opportunity for the realization of its objective and development. Hence, it moves to another location where opportunities for growth and development are more abundant. In another instance, the corporate citizen, like a private individual, loves its birthplace with a passion so great that if the place is not all that it could be, the citizen will do all that is possible to help the birthplace realize its full potential.

Maybe it is destined to become a shining example of corporate commitment by improving its surroundings and becoming a good citizen in the community of its central location. A corporation seems, at times, to develop a personality after a series of like management, each leaving a legacy of dedication to the community and its development. But what is more remarkable is the contagious effect this type of dedication and commitment has on other corporations and businesses that relocates to the area.

The area to which I refer is Atlanta; the corporation is Coca-Cola.

If Atlanta helped to launch Coca-Cola, she also reaped benefits a thousand-fold. Atlanta and the Coca-Cola Corporation are almost irrevocably tied together and thrive as one. Each succeeding generation of founders and stockholders have had strong ties to the continuing success and growth of the city and is its most generous benefactor. I have a sneaking suspicion that every C.E.O. must take an oath, honor and promise to do everything in his power as officer and individual to promote and give support to all worthwhile efforts of the city of Atlanta, so help him God. This was, of course, in addition to increasing his corporate skill and technical know-how.

As a result of this dedication and interest in the city, a corporate network existed in the city that had great influence throughout Georgia. It is not only economic influence, but a vast quiet political influence, all directed toward making Atlanta the greatest, most prosperous and racially peaceful city in the world.

Realizing the importance of education, corporations are most generous in their support of all public and private educational institutions, and any campaign for funds not only are assured success, but frequently exceed their goals. It is inconceivable to think of a united appeal campaign for any of the many red feather agencies not headed by a C.E.O. of one of the major corporations. Corporations have been known to release a corporate executive to give full-time efforts for the duration of the campaign.

Atlanta is fortunate in being the headquarters of a number of charitable foundations, well-funded and expertly managed. They work closely together and are centrally administered by a professional who recommends from time to time the most pressing or desirable needs of the city - educational, cultural, or simply replacing a public eyesore with a mid-city park on what may be the most expensive piece of real estate in the city.

In most instances, this unity and cooperation among the charitable foundations have a common source for their affluence. It was the corporation that adopted the city and created more individual and collective wealth than any other known investment. Aggressive management that merchandises its products on a world-wide basis invokes the envy and respect of the corporate world. It is no less protective of its products than of its corporation integrity and its devotion and dedication to the city of its birth.

To assure the continuity of a wholesome and viable community and well-run government, locally and statewide, the corporation does not divorce itself from political interest. That interest can be very vital to aspirants of public office.

It is important to know how the system works and to know how and where the decisions are made. There is no formal organization, like the Chamber of Commerce, which would have input by the very nature of its membership. The consensus comes through a unique network or lines of communication that stretches through all of the financial institutions, private membership clubs, and CEOs of the major corporations. This is significant because the bottom line is economic vitality, supported by a strong educational and cultural environment. The benevolence of this coalition is what makes and keeps Atlanta progressive and attractive as a refreshing oasis to newcomers and natives alike.

Their support is not entirely indispensable to political or economic success. On the other hand, to have their blessings seems to assist in dispensing with some of the usual problems, financial and otherwise.

In the past, there existed a similar political and economic

coalition, in the minority community which, in most instances, tended to emulate to a lessor degree the majority citizens. A degree of cooperation between the Black and White community has been invaluable to helping Atlanta to avoid much of the unpleasantness and problems of desegregation of schools and public places.

Negotiation rather than confrontation has been the pattern of solving or seeking equitable solutions to any racial problem. On one occasion involving housing in a boarder line neighborhood, a newcomer from above "Smith and Western" didn't know this. He began to beat on the table and make remarks foreign to our usual meetings. Everybody looked at him as he raved over what will not be permitted, and someone said to him, that isn't how we solve our differences down here. He was a corporate transplant to a local office.

The word got around that he was undesirable to Atlanta, and unceremoniously he was removed by his corporation, never to be heard of again in Atlanta. More so in Atlanta than other cities, it is not good to unnecessarily cross words with the corporate coalition.

You don't usually think of a city as having a personality or other characteristics attributed to individuals. However, native Atlantans have a tendency to describe their city as they would a person that is progressive, lively, friendly, a bit arrogant, widely diversified economically, and so on. As to its reaction to persons or situations, one could add, it can be benevolent or positive. Never boastful in its benevolence nor ruthless with its punishment.

If an individual or organization's actions are adverse to what is conceded to be good for the city and its citizens, they may find themselves isolated from any community worthwhile benefits. If on the other hand, misfortune falls upon one whose contributions and interest in the city has been demonstrated, relief and help is almost a certainty. There is a safety net that will appear to break the fall in the form of new opportunities for recovery. The love, respect, and devotion must run both ways to achieve this effective relationship.

Epilogue

Success may be delayed, but it is no Citadel of Immunity from failure.

T.M.Alexander, Sr.

If you are going some place you have never been, it is good judgement to decide ahead of time why you want to go and the reason for choosing one place over others. The route should be mapped and a time schedule determined, making allowances for unexpected but unavoidable delays. Also, there should be a well-designed program for the arrival.

If a road map is necessary for a long trip, it is much more essential for a life and a career. One must have a goal to shoot for and not face life aimlessly, leaving destiny to the fickleness of fate.

Delayed dreams are not always denials. Sometimes we have to be tested to see whether we have the strength, courage, and character to treat success as a blessing, and as a responsibility rather than a citadel of immunity from sharing and serving others. Sometimes we have to go through what the biblical Job experienced before obtaining ultimate happiness.

Job considered himself a good, honest person of integrity and a good citizen and family man. He was so fortunate that his friends and associates thought he was shielded with divine protection from harm or failure. Eventually God tested Job to demonstrate that his faith was unshakable. Only those who have experienced the loss of loved ones children gone, friends strength and understanding hardly sufficient to sustain him, material resources vanished, body weak, and heart broken.

When he was urged by friends to abandon that *mustard seed faith that could move mountains*, Job said, "No. Even though He slays me, still do I trust Him." Job had every reason to give up and die, but he was being saved for a purpose, and that purpose required the strength and courage to withstand the difficulties life sometimes imposes upon us.

Later, his losses were replaced, and strength and life were awarded him. Job prospered and found happiness and joy in service to others beyond himself. He had found love and peace beyond understanding.

A Road Map For Faith and Patience

There is no chance, no destiny, no fate,
That can circumvent, hinder, or control
The firm resolve of a determined soul.
Gifts count for nothing, only will is great!
What power can stay the force
Of a sea-seeking river in its mighty course,
Or cause the ascending orb of day to stand and wait?
Each well-borne soul must win what it deserves,
Whose actions and inaction serves the one great end.
Even death will stand still and wait an hour or two on
such a will!"

T.M. Alexander, Sr.

My friend and mentor on all that is spiritual was the late Howard Thurman. Whenever I had the opportunity I just sat and listened to him. He shared many of his experiences with me and was the source of strength I could call on from what he taught. He said, "The reason we call God, Father, is that you can talk to Him as you would your papa in times of trouble or when needed. You could even question Him, and He would hear you with tongue in cheek, but never forsake you."

I followed Thurman's philosophy wherever I could. It worked so quickly to meet my needs it was frightening, not only throughout my life, but during one of the darkest periods of my life.

My wife Dorothy and I had been happily married for more than 40 years. I will never forget the trust and faith she put in me when she gave up her scholarship to Spelman College to become my wife. I lived up to my promise to her and eventually gave her anything she asked for.

She endowed me with the responsibility that I needed in my life, something which my mother long ago had realized. Dorothy helped discipline me and keep me firm to my path. Over the years, we traveled extensively, both here in America and in Europe. Together, we watched and participated in great global conflicts, stirring political movements, and the nurturing of our family. When she died, my spirit sought to flee frantically with hers. I lay deathly ill for a period of time after my dear wife's passing. I asked God to give me a quick reason for keeping me alive or to just take me away. My grief was so deep.

I had an answer in 24 hours.

Through a chance encounter, I found Lenora, who was destined to fill a much needed void in my life. I met Lenora through a friend of the family. Over a period of time, we got to know each other through long telephone conversations and visits. Lenora, a successful professional woman in her own right, had similar attitudes toward life and purpose. Lenora had patience, understanding, and caring. She brought harmony and meaning back to my life, thus allowing me to continue on my unfinished program. Because of her, I could stay the course, even when the way was rough. I thank God for Lenora.

Also, I thank God for my offspring. My children and grandchildren have given me no cause to worry. The foundation I and others have laid down will greatly serve my children's feet so that they in turn can lay down more foundation for the ones following them. Their futures seem destined to live up to the legacy and heritage of their proud and very successful ancestors.

Success, a hope to achieve a goal during our life time, is something we all dream of frequently. Whatever may be our occupation or profession, the ultimate objective is to wear the crown of success. However, success must be constantly won. It is a level of responsibility in which we are obligated to make good. To capture the crown of success requires constantly raising challenges over our heads to keep us growing taller and more responsive to the obligations achievement imposes upon us. I first chose business as a career in which to succeed, never realizing that what makes one successful in one sphere can lead to service and possible success in another.

It is said that, if an artist looks at his work of art with complete satisfaction and considers it perfect, he will never create a better work. If a musician listens to his last composition and considers it a masterpiece of perfection, he will never compose a great symphony. It is the utter dissatisfaction with one's accomplishments, and the disturbing realization that success must be continuously won, but never admittedly achieved, that is the key to progress.

It is so easy to become overwhelmed with one's major and minor triumphs, particularly when we achieve against what seems like all odds. However, an instrument cannot become sharp on a soft stone. Facing difficulties seem to make us invincible, and often we are closest to victory when defeated in a noble cause.

Success is relative. Success can be attributed to one person by another, only if you are privy to that person's objective. What may appear to a casual observer as success, may be a miserable failure to the person involved. It is for that reason we should be careful in attributing success to an individual who has, according to our personal standards, obtained a position we envy. Similarly, it is also true that acclaim by others, can sometimes make a person either abandon or modify his objectives or dreams for success.

Too often, all of us at one time or another have been guilty of over estimating our strength and influence and adopting an imperial attitude. In other words, we suffer with a case of mistaken identity. Our attitudes toward individuals and situations gives the impression of authoritative, undisputable correctness and righteousness of whatever position we take.

In my experience in the community, I have seen the mighty and exalted tumble from their pinnacle of self-sufficiency. We should avoid becoming beside ourselves, remembering, *to whom much is given, much is required.* One may, like a wild stream, overrun its banks, and cause torrential destruction in its wake. However, there can be a gully in the land, a shape to the external hills or declivity in the valley that directs the wildest stream not to the channel that it chose, but one that nature and God did. Therefore, do not think more of yourself than you ought to. Humanity is a virtue, arrogance a sin.

Whether in business or politics, the ultimate objective should be service. If one serves the community, and contributes to its growth and progress, personal success is the by-product. To try to achieve personal success at the expense and disregard of the welfare of others will lead to eventual failure. To retain a level of self-respect and reasonable security, one must constantly strengthen and reinforce the foundation beneath oneself. No one can long survive in isolation or oblivion to his fellows and his community. Even when your motives are not unselfish, the only way you can remain secure in your satisfied status, on top of the heap, is to continually strengthen the foundation beneath your feet. In other words, you can not attain or sustain success in any venture in utter disregard to the true sources of power and support.

Atlanta did not spring fully developed as we will see it today, from the head of Zeus who ruled from Mt. Olympus, according to Greek mythology. It was founded in 1837 as the terminus of Western and Atlantic Railroad. It was also a major supply center during the Civil War and was burned to the ground by Union forces in 1864. Its leadership rapidly rebuilt the city, laying the foundation for the major commercial and financial center for the South Atlantic States.

Realizing the importance of education, leadership established more than twenty colleges and universities. Atlanta is the gateway to the South, the southern and international distribution point for products and services for corporations and governments on a world-wide basis. The city's own products and services are likewise limitless to foreign and domestic consumption.

In the scheme of things, the history of Black Atlanta's relatively world-wide achievements was the result of the efforts of a few pioneers. The Black Atlantans' strategy for survival first involved seeking out the decision makers and power brokers in the community and determining the nature of their intentions.

Luckily, as I grew in business in the 1930s, there developed a White leadership that not only wanted to build Atlanta, but also to lessen or do away with segregation and discrimination. Chief among this more benevolent leadership was that found at Coca-Cola.

Throughout the struggle to desegregate, White and Black leadership decided to cooperate. As time went by, sitting down with each other became easier, once each group became known and respected by the other group both individually and collectively. Consensus building was what we were about before the name was applied. Because of the efforts of individuals, those who dared to dream, there is a homogeneous quality of boisterousness among citizens of Atlanta and it is contagious. Newcomers catch it very quickly and those few who build up a resistance to it find little comfort and company, personally or in the corporate community.

With all of this going for Atlanta and the emergence of new dynamic bi-racial young leadership, caution is in order. There is a natural tendency to relax vigilance when everything seems to move in your favor. There is nothing so certain as the element of risk, and there is nothing more risky than the unpredictable, from natural and unnatural forces.

Nevertheless, I have faith that Atlanta will survive, especially if we remember the bridges that brought us over, and those who cleared the debris in the path to a truly bi-racial system where friendship and fellowship among groups are seen as a plus. This certainly has been my life's position. The kind of fellowship necessary to run anything smoothly required us to do certain things.

Therefore, I repeat for emphasis:

*Remember to speak to those as we go up the escalator to success, because we might meet them on our way down. Live **in**, instead of **off** your community. Wisdom and strength will under-gird the foundation upon which you can build and help ensure the success and progress for which all people should strive.*

Alexander's Creed
for
Business Success

Success in business is not only determined by the level of financial acquisition, but also by the type of person one becomes in pursuit of it. Develop these character traits steadfastly. They contributed to my success and will certainly contribute to yours.

Trust

The basis for developing a strategy of survival or road map is to create an atmosphere of trust and confidence in everything with which you are associated. What may appear to be a popular opinion or view may not necessarily be sound or valid. Remember what my papa taught me: Anything you get wrong, you won't have for long.

Stick To Your Principles

In business, when all else fails, one must be guided by principles. On occasion, worthiness of the cause outweighs the risk required to support it. Stand.

Community Involvement

Associate yourself with worthwhile causes in the community. Be counted among those who are building a sound and durable foundation for growth, development, or improvement. Live **in** the community, and not **on** it.

Respect Yourself

Never ask of your friends or associates anything they cannot grant with honor and self-respect. Likewise, never take a position or act in a way that reflects poorly on your character or diminishes your self-respect or credibility in your own eyes or in the eyes of others.

Be Yourself

One thing is basic: Be, in reality, all that you appear to be. Don't give the impression of being anything but yourself. That is precisely what you have got to deal with, live with and manage, for better or worse, the rest of your life. Anything else is the height of hypocrisy. Your real self in the nature of things will eventually surface.

Be Dependable

Maintain and insist on a high degree of professional integrity and self-respect. By all means be dependable. Let it be known, by example, that you can be relied upon to live up to any promise or commitment you make. As the old saying goes, "Say what you mean, and mean what you say."

Respect Others

Respect the opinions and limitations of others, whether they are in agreement with your own or not. No one has a monopoly on what is absolute truth. It is a good sign of self-examination to pursue what you do not know, and realize that others have answers to what may be questions to you.

Listen More, Speak Less

Don't be ashamed to ask for help where you need it, no matter what you need. You can increase your knowledge and efficiency by more listening and less talking.

Focus On Your Goal

It is important to keep your ultimate objective clearly focused before you so that every step taken will lead to the achievement of your dreams and aspirations. Hold on to your dreams and ambitions. Do not diminish them to accommodate the limited view of others who may feel that your plans and goals cannot be reached.

Rely On Your Special Talents And Skills

Finally, do not try to build the foundation to your dreams with borrowed tools. Do as David did against the evil giant. Stick to your slingshot and rocks, and leave armor and sword to Saul. Goliath is the enemy who is in your path to success and victory. Face him with the weapons you know best, tried and proven by your own skills. This I learned to do as Thurman would say, **"Beyond the Timberline."**

A Legacy of Service and Commitment

Theodore Martin (T.M.) Alexander, Sr.

By Janice A. Davis

Economics, and its impact on business and the community, is a subject that many people do not understand. T.M. Alexander not only understands the subject - he has been a major contributor to its redefinition during the 20th Century.

T.M.'s company insured the Civil Rights movement from the Bus Boycott in Montgomery to the March on Washington. He was the first to recognize the need for providing financial support for Dr. Martin Luther King, Jr., through insurance on King and his aides. This level of foresight was fully supported by the "invisible" structure that, through T.M.'s influence, sanctioned not only the Civil Rights Movement, but also gave full support to later achievements that involved all Americans. In 1957, he opened the door for Blacks to run for public office in the South, by being the first Black to run in the City of Atlanta since the Civil War.

In areas of housing, T.M. supervised the building of one of the first upper middle-class Black subdivisions. This opened the door to home ownership for the Black family with a larger income base.

T.M. is truly a pioneer in our time and one who has shaped the future in a very positive way. There is a very critical need for the development of a series of biographical data on people of T.M.'s area of expertise and a need for the historical review of the impact of their contribution to true economic development. This need exists, because during the past two decades a void has developed that has forced the new generations to loose touch with the reality of struggle, which serves as the very foundation for the freedoms which people presently take for granted.

This publication addresses a true re-definition and a realistic view of our capitalistic system. Through this autobiographical work, we can experience the development, progress, and impact that history had in shaping the economic condition of the minority community and how this development has expanded and strengthened the entire economic and social base of America.

Theodore Martin Alexander, Sr., played a critical role in the "evolution" of America. This autobiography provides an important literary reference to his contribution.

PROFILE

Known in Georgia as "Mr. Insurance," Theodore Martin (T.M.) Alexander, Sr., founded Alexander & Company in 1931. The company grew to become one of the nations oldest and most successful minority owned independent insurance agencies serving major corporate businesses and institutions throughout the United States.

In addition to insurance, T.M. and his associates formed other businesses in the areas of real estate development, banking, and social establishments. Key among these were the Southeastern Fidelity Fire and Casualty Company formed in 1951, and Alexander and Colloway, a real estate development firm. Southeastern Fidelity provided more than $50 million of property protection for its clients and was the first Black owned multi-line insurance company. The real estate firm developed land and constructed apartment buildings and individuals homes. Most notable is the 127 apartment unit in the center of Atlanta University on more than five acres of land.

Recognizing the absence of Black representation in electoral politics in both the City of Atlanta and the State of Georgia, T.M. embarked upon an ambitious effort and ran for City Alderman in 1957 and the State Senate in 1961. His campaign sparked racial unrest and he was not elected to office. However, the tone, character, and execution of his campaigns were considered above reproach throughout the entire ordeal. His efforts were recognized by both the White and Black communities as having paved the way for other Blacks to become elected officials throughout the South.

T.M. Alexander, Sr., has been in the forefront of important developments in the social, political, and economic sectors and has held numerous distinctions and affiliations including...

- Partner and Chairman, MARTA (Metropolitan Atlanta Rapid Transit Authority) Insurance Managers

- Listed in Who's Who in America

- Secretary and Member of Executive Committee and Board of Trustees of Morehouse College

- Member of Executive Committee and Board of Atlanta University Center Corporation

- Former Member of the Board and Secretary-Treasurer of Mutual Federal Savings and Loan Association

- Member of the Board of Directors, Blue Cross & Blue Shield of Greater Atlanta

- Member of the Board of Directors of the African Development Foundation (Presidential appointment confirmed by the Senate)

- Former member of Community Relations Commission of Atlanta

- Former Chairman of the Board of the Butler Street YMCA, and member of the Executive Committee

- Former Vice Chairman of the City of Atlanta Ethics Committee

- Former Chairman of the Citizens Advisory Committee of Urban Renewal and Development, Atlanta

- Former member of the Executive Committee and Assistant Treasurer of the Atlanta Community Chest

- Former Chairman of the Board of Senior Citizens of Metropolitan Atlanta

- Member of Sigma Pi Phi National Fraternity of professional men distinguished in their professions

- Member of Atlanta Chamber of Commerce

- Member of Atlanta Association of Independent Insurance Agents

- Member, Alpha Phi Alpha Fraternity

- Charter member of the National Association of Real Estate Brokers

- Member of the Board of Directors of Boys' Clubs of Greater Washington, DC

- Member of the Council of 100 Black Republicans

He attended high school at Morehouse Academy in Atlanta and graduated with honors from Morehouse College with a degree in Business Administration. He received an Honorary Doctor of Law degree from Morehouse in 1970. He has also served as an Adjunct Professor of Insurance at Howard University in Washington, D.C. He now devotes his time to writing, speaking, and consulting.

Born in Montgomery, Alabama in 1909, T.M. Alexander, Sr., now holds residences in Atlanta, Georgia and Washington, D.C. He is married to Dr. Lenora Cole-Alexander, former Director of the Women's Bureau of the U.S. Department of Labor. She is currently President of LCA and Associates, Inc., and Commonwealth Professor of Public Affairs at George Mason University.

INDEX

A

Abernathy, Ralph, 214, 217, 224
Academies, black, 31
Achieving goals in life, 12-15
Action Forum, 227
Adamsville, 165
Adversity, 11
  overcoming, 11
Aiken, Walter, 137, 151, 171
Alexander and Company, 137
  start of, 86-96
Alexander, James Henry, 19
Alexander-Calloway Realty Co., 235
Allen, John S., 151
Alpha Phi Alpha, 119
Alston, J.A., 152
American Home Mission Board, 58
America's Tenth Man: A Pictorial Review... 137
Amos, Dr. Rufus, 173
Associated Enterprises, 137
Association of Southern Women
  Against Lynching, 172
Atlanta Constitution, The, 160, 172
Atlanta Daily World, 138
Atlanta, Georgia,
  black and white coalition
    building, 228-232
  black housing development, 155
  corporate support, 241-244
  early black business leaders, 58
  history of, 56-60
Atlanta Life Insurance Co., 32, 153
Atlanta Negro Chamber of
  Commerce, 122
Atlanta University, 32, 58, 106

B

Bankers Fire Insurance Co., 71, 80

Bell, O.T., 151
Beyond The Timberline, 14
Bickers, J.T., 152
Blacks, and the Republican
  Party, 171-172
Black bank, first, 57
Black burial associations, 57
Black businesses,
  before 20th century, 57
  in Atlanta, 32, 57-60
Black business leaders,
  early black business leaders of
    Atlanta, 58-60
Black housing,
  expansion patterns, 153
  in Atlanta, 149-170
Black life, early,
  acquisition of property, 74
  conditions after World War 1, 35
  conditions in the North, 37
  dominating building trades, 18
  moving to the North, 34
Black life insurance companies,
  start of, 57
Black property and casualty
  insurance, 73-75
Blacks, political interests,
  after Civil War, 158
Blacks, southern, 9
Blacks, treatment of, 32
Blayton, Jesse B., 45, 58, 81,
Brown, Charlotte Hawkins, 136
Bus Boycott, The, 215, 255
Business and Our Tomorrow, 138
Butler Street YMCA, 114, 115

C

Caldwell, Allen, 152
Calloway Realty, 137